My Encounters with Angels & Other Memoirs

by

MARJORIE J. REED

Marjorie

may God bless you

Merry Christmas 2016   Sister Reed is now Blind. It's hard for her to write. But my writing's not much better   Love Sis Rachael

Copyright © 2015 Marjorie J. Reed

All rights reserved.

Cover Design by Delia Latham

Unless otherwise specified, Scripture quotations are from the King James Version of the Bible.

All rights reserved. No portion of this publication may be reproduced, stored, or transmitted in any form or by any means without written permission of the publisher or its entities.

This book is based on the memories and experiences of the author. All persons mentioned, either living or dead, incidents, locales, and dialog are based on the author's recollections only. Any inconsistencies, inaccuracies, or mistakes are solely the result of human error and should not be attributed to historical fact.

DEDICATION

I dedicate this book to my husband John and each one of our girls: Lois, Leona, Mary, and Rebecca. Hopefully the stories in this book will live in your memories for a long time. My greatest desire in writing it is that you will be reminded to always put God first in your lives. He has a plan for each one of you.

When I look around the Marriage Supper of the Lamb, I don't want any of our family to be missing. I have loved each one of you with all my heart.

To my dear husband John, I didn't know when I married you that I could love anyone so completely as I have you. I appreciate all your patience with me and hearing you say, "I love you," and showing it daily.

Lois and Leona, not only did God give your daddy and me to each other, but he included the two of you as well. I have loved you both with all my heart.

Mary Owenna, we named you after both of your grandmothers. Mary Steffy Powell and Owenna Elliott Reed. I couldn't have named you after any others who were more dedicated to the Lord. Their lives were excellent examples for you to follow, and you didn't lack for love. Now I depend on you more than ever to take care of my daily needs. You never complain. Thanks, honey.

Rebecca Rose, you were our miracle baby. You filled such an empty place in our home after your brother Tommy's death. From the beginning, you were our little songbird. God's hand has been upon you, and you have been an inspiration to everyone who knows you. I have had to lean on your shoulders many times and still do.

ACKNOWLEDGMENTS

This book was made possible with labor and love by Nikki Denney, who felt led by the Lord to help me collect my memoirs and assemble them here. Nikki, may God's blessings always be upon your life. Thank you so much for everything you've done.

God provided a miracle only he could do when I was introduced to Teresa Slack. Teresa is a fiction writer who has published several novels and short stories, and attends church with us. Without her willingness to invest the monumental amount of time and work involved in bringing all my thoughts, dreams, and experiences together, I doubt this book ever would've made it to market. Teresa, you have been a beacon of light to me through this process. You are truly one of my miracles.

I wish to thank Carolyn Butcher and Delia Latham for their help with the formatting and editing process. I didn't know where to begin with inserting pictures into text or setting the project up for publication. They jumped in and solved all those problems for me. Carolyn helped Mary and Teresa put together the images for the cover that best depicted the vision the Lord showed me the day he told me I would write this book. Delia took that beautiful artwork and created the cover of the book you are now holding in your hands. I am pleased beyond measure with the finished product and want to thank everyone involved from the bottom of my heart.

I also want to thank my cousin, Olive Thompson, who helped me continuously as I worked on this book. Our daughter, Mary Owenna, has also been a huge help to me. She ran errands, looked up dates, fact checked, copied pictures and poems, edited during our many read-throughs and always provided lunch for Teresa and me during our writing sessions, even though she was working just as hard. Thank you so much, Mary, for your tireless efforts.

INTRODUCTION

And Jesus looking upon them saith, With men it is impossible, but not with God: for with God all things are possible. –Mark 10:27

My mother gave me my first diary when I was a young girl after she realized how much I enjoyed writing. I have kept diaries most of my life. Expressing my thoughts and feelings through writing came naturally to me. After our family devotions were over in the evening and everyone else was in bed, I would take advantage of the quiet time to record what happened that day. Believe me, there was always so much to write in a day's time when you had nine brothers.

Keeping a journal soon became more than just recording everyday events and thoughts that seemed important at the time. It has been a great comfort to me over the years as I worked through things on my mind. Anytime God gave me something special, I wanted to write it down right away before I forgot it. I wanted to share some of these things with others. Other things though, I kept private to mull over as I walked with the Lord. My journal writings were always helpful as I prepared to speak to a ladies' group or to a church in the ministry I shared with my husband John.

Since no one on earth knows more about me than I do, I wanted to share a bit of my life, as well as tell the stories of the angels I have encountered. There are many stories from my life recorded in the following pages no one has ever heard—some sad, some joyous, some tragic, and some amusing.

Dear reader, I pray you are inspired and encouraged by the story of my life. I want God's anointing to be on each copy of this book and on each pair of hands that hold it. I believe it will be so. My greatest desire is for you to read something within these pages that will touch your heart for good, and you will know it is real. I pray the stories in this book will help you work through issues in your own life. Most of all, I pray it stirs a longing in your heart to draw closer to our Heavenly Father who has a purpose for each and every one of us. May the Lord bless you mightily as you read.

As for my brothers and family, I pray you will be reminded of some of the things that happened to us while we were growing up, and it will bring joy and happiness to you.

Please remember, the following stories are based solely on my memories. Memory is never perfect, so some of the stories or dialog may not be recorded as they actually happened. For that, I apologize. I wrote this book to the best of my ability, with the Lord's help during every step, and I pray for your patience and understanding.

MY VISION FOR THIS BOOK

When I first realized I was legally blind, I asked God to take me home.

It was January 2012. Outside my window, the world was blanketed in pristine white, but I barely noticed. Seated on the couch in my living room, I wondered if God still had a plan for my life. I was old and tired. I could barely see. What could I do for the Kingdom of God? I couldn't imagine how God would use me at this point in my life.

I suppose a lot of people have felt this way at some time or another. But it had never happened to me. All my life I had been the one others turned to, the one others leaned on when times got tough. For the first time in my life, I faced the reality that I had become a burden to my family.

My husband John had been sick for a long time. I had taken care of him for eight years. Now that I was legally blind, how would I continue to take care of him? What would become of us?

The more I thought about it, the more despondent I became. I felt like I was coming to the end of myself. My sight was growing progressively worse. There were days I couldn't see well enough to cook our meals. My health and strength were failing. I just wanted the Lord to take me home. That seemed like the only way to keep from becoming a burden to my daughters or anyone else.

As I pondered these thoughts in my mind, God gave me the vision for this book.

One afternoon there was no one in the house but John and me. Earlier in the day, I had been holding his hand and singing to him. He was in very poor health at this point. Every day before he fell asleep he would say, "I love you more than words can say." He had told me these words every day of our marriage. God had truly blessed me with a wonderful husband.

After John dozed off, I went to the couch and sat down.

I had only been sitting there a few moments when a bluish cloud appeared and seemed to fill the room. It was the most beautiful shade of blue I had ever seen. Everything else in the room faded from view as the blue cloud filled the room. A white cloud appeared to my right. Out of that cloud came a voice like nothing I had heard before. I knew immediately it was the voice of God speaking directly to me. I felt the power of God cover me while I was sitting on the couch. It was so strong that for days afterward, I could still feel his presence. That's how I knew it was real. It wasn't something my mind thought up on its own.

The Lord said to me, "You will write a book."

I could hardly believe my ears. My dream since I was a child had been to write a book. That dream had never come true. Yet here I was at age eighty-five; a tired, old, legally blind woman at the end of her rope, and God was telling me to write a book.

Not only did God tell me I was going to write a book, he gave me a vision of what the book would look like, including the title and my name as the author. It was crystal clear to my eyes, even though it had been ages since I could see well enough to read a regularly printed book. The vision of that cover is as close to what you are holding now as I could make it.

At that moment, the Lord's glory manifested in a warm, precious, soothing light that filled the entire room. The glory of God's presence was so great. Words cannot express how it made me feel. The joy of the Lord engulfed me as I sat there on the couch and took in his message to me. Just as suddenly as the vision appeared, it was gone.

God *was* going to use me. He still had a purpose for me in my advanced years, though I wasn't sure how any of it would happen. Writing a book was such a huge undertaking. I didn't think I was up to the task. Nevertheless, I didn't doubt the vision or the Lord's ability to carry me through.

I've always wanted to give God my best, and I want to have something to give back when my life is over. I longed to do everything his way. I sure didn't want the Lord to take me before I finished this book.

Though writing a book at my age and with my limitations seemed impossible, I knew God had a reason for it. When he asks us to do something that looks impossible, he will make it possible.

Needless to say I wanted to know more. How would I write a book when I couldn't see and had never used a computer? After the book was finished, how would I make it available to readers? I knew nothing about editing or publication or putting a book on the market.

Later that day, I told John about what the Lord had shown me. He said, "How can you write a book? You can't even cross your T's and dot your I's."

He had always teased me about my handwriting.

After I received the Lord's instruction to write this book, I couldn't wait to get started. I have served the Lord since I was eight-years-old, and I always tried to obey him. I knew writing a book would be hard work and outside my comfort zone, but I wanted to walk in complete obedience to him. More than anything, I pray the words written in this book will point every reader to God, knowing that whatever he tells us to do, no matter how impossible it looks, he will make a way.

I didn't know it at the time, but God had already begun working in the heart of one of my dear sisters in the Lord, Nikki Denney. Years earlier I had taught Nikki's mother in my Sunday School class when she was a little girl. Nikki and her husband Shane, who is a pastor, often came to visit John while he was sick. They always brought words of encouragement and would pray with us.

I was a little cautious about telling people about my vision. I knew it was from God, but sometimes it's best not to tell everything until the right time. The next time Nikki and Shane came to visit, I told her about my vision. Right away she offered to help. I hardly knew Nikki before that day. I was so surprised by her offer. We both believed the Lord had brought us together. This really inspired us to begin our work. I could feel the witness between us. Nikki became my eyes, and she would do the writing for me. Every time she had a chance between church work and her usual daily chores, she came to the house to help me work on the book. I could not have asked for anyone more dedicated to start my book.

During the night, God would generally give me what to write the following day. Always when it was quiet, his spirit would come upon me and tell me what to tell Nikki the next day when she came to write. Each moment spent in his presence was glorious. It seemed like I was sitting at the Lord's feet waiting on his instruction.

And all things, whatsoever you shall ask in prayer, believing, you shall receive. -Matthew 21:22

Over the next few months Nikki and I worked on the book, recording many stories from my childhood growing up in a family with nine little brothers. I shared with Nikki my encounters with angels and the many ways the Lord moved in my life and the life of John and our girls.

It wasn't long before Nikki and I reached the point where we couldn't go any further. We had recorded much of my story, but we didn't have a clue how to turn my thoughts and experiences into a publishable book. It was then that another dear friend, Melissa Hammit, told Teresa Slack that I needed help finishing my book and preparing it for publication. Teresa showed up at the house one day, and we went to work. With her help and the help of my daughter, Mary, we were able to fulfill the purpose the Lord put on my heart when he told me I would write this book.

Many other wonderful people have contributed to getting my book ready for print. You probably won't know this side of glory just how much your help and patience have meant to me as I fulfilled the purpose the Lord put on my heart.

Marjorie with her good friend, Nikki Denney and Nikki's husband Shane.

CHAPTER ONE

Stories of my Grandparents

In 1910 my mother's parents, Charles and Cora Steffy, decided to go west to North Dakota to homestead. Grandpa Steffy was adventurous to say the least. He never did anything on a small scale. He and Cora loaded all their family belongings into a covered wagon, including five children ranging in age from thirteen to my mother Mary, who was only five-months-old at the time, and headed west.

It was November when they headed out and already turning cold. It was important for the family to complete the trip before winter hit. Winter arrived early in North Dakota.

When they reached the Mississippi River, they loaded as many of their belongings as they could onto a barge. There was too much for one trip so Charles and Cora left the older children, along with Monta who was five and Katherine who was two and a half, on the riverbank with strict orders to stay put until the adults returned for them.

The children were so excited as they watched the barge leave the dock. They waved and jumped up and down in delight. Five-year-old Monta took off her hat and waved it in the air. Katherine lunged for the hat. Monta had been taught to share with her little sister, but with Mother on the barge and the older children not paying attention to what she was doing, she held the hat out of Katherine's reach. Katherine's lower lip jutted out.

Monta knew Mother wouldn't be pleased when she came back if she found Katherine's eyes red and puffy from crying. Begrudgingly, Monta relented and set the hat on Katherine's head.

Katherine sure did look cute wearing a hat that was much too big for her. She waved at the barge so Mother would see how pretty she looked with Monta's hat on her head. The barge had edged away from the dock, and Mother and Father weren't looking at her in her pretty hat. Katherine stepped closer to the edge of the bank.

The older children were still watching the barge and all the interesting activity going on at the dock. No one was looking at Katherine. If only she could get Mother's attention one more time.

"Mama," she called out. She stepped closer to the water's edge and waved the hat over her head the way Monta had done. The hat slipped out of her hands and into the water. Without another thought, she jumped into the cold water after the hat. If the water could carry the heavy barge across the water, it could certainly keep one little girl afloat while she reclaimed her hat.

From her spot onboard the barge, Cora saw Katherine go into the water. "Save my baby! Save my baby!" she screamed with her heart in her throat.

God must've honored Cora's desperate pleas. Katherine's pantaloons instantly filled with air, and she began floating downstream. The small group ran along the shore keeping pace with the bobbing little girl, while the barge pilot stopped the barge and brought it back to the dock. Katherine floated until she came to some limbs and trash next to the bank where her clothes snagged on a tree. A young man was the first to reach her. He ran into the water and snatched her free and handed her back to her crying mother.

The rest of the trip was relatively uneventful, much to the relief of Cora who kept little Katherine close by. The family kept traveling westward until they reached North Dakota where some of Grandpa Steffy's cousins lived on a wide open prairie. The landscape stretched for miles as far as they could see without a hill to slow the relentless wind. Accustomed to the rolling hills of southern Ohio, the flat expanse of the North Dakota prairie was more than they had bargained for. Even the adventurous Grandpa Steffy wasn't sure he could endure more than one winter on the prairie.

If they built a house and homesteaded for a certain length of time, the government would give them a deed to the property, so Grandpa Steffy dug in his heels, determined to stay.

The family lived that first winter with Grandpa Steffy's cousins in a dugout house while they waited for the opportunity to begin homesteading on their own. The family made friends with a little Indian girl from the Dakota tribe. Her name was hard for the children to pronounce so they simply called her "Dakota". Everyone in the family loved it when she came to visit. She had her own pony, and she could ride like the wind. She taught them things that proved very helpful. The Indians showed Cora how to carry Mary like a papoose so she could keep her hands free while she was working.

One day Cora made some loaves of yeast bread. The delicious aroma wafted into the fields and got Dakota's attention. When Grandma finished baking the bread, she gave Dakota a loaf. The young girl was so pleased by the gift she hugged Cora so tightly Cora thought she broke a couple ribs.

The family had many fond memories of their time in North Dakota, but Grandpa Steffy realized he wasn't suited for prairie life. Everyone missed their home and family in southern Ohio and moved back in the spring of 1911.

They brought back with them a dog that was part wolf. The dog had boundless energy so the children named him Bounce. Anytime Grandma or Grandpa Steffy tried to correct the children, Bounce would grab the hand that held the switch and not let go until they dropped it. The kids loved Bounce's trick, but Grandpa Steffy wasn't as enthused. Still, he let the children keep Bounce. The dog was their hero.

Grandpa Powell

My dad's father, Byrd Powell was small in stature but big in every other way. He had a rough time growing up. His mother died when he was five-years-old. There were a few older children in the family, but his father didn't think he could take care of a little boy. Byrd was sent to live with at least five different families, but he kept finding his way back home.

His father eventually married a Christian wife who loved children. Little Byrd's new stepmother had a soft heart and was more patient with a precocious little boy than her husband. Life improved considerably for little Byrd after that.

He showed musical talent from an early age. When he got older, he played the fiddle for barn dances and delivered moonshine to people. However, after he gave his heart to the Lord, he never delivered moonshine or picked up his fiddle again. He would say, "I played for the devil, but I don't want any strings attached when I come into the church."

After he came to know the Lord, he was one of the happiest people you ever met.

Byrd could not read or write, and he never learned to drive. He rode mules or walked wherever he wanted to go. He would not own a horse. He wanted mules. The southern Ohio terrain was hilly, and mules were more sure-footed and useful on a farm. When the Powells moved to Ohio from Jackson County, Kentucky, they came in a wagon pulled by mules. They lived in Hamilton for a period of time. Byrd knew he wanted to live in the country and have a dairy farm.

He and my grandmother, Mary Ellen Wells, found a farm in Oregonia, Ohio along the Little Miami River. The farm was in a valley in a beautiful area Indians had once prized as their favorite hunting ground. As soon as Byrd found the property, he sought the Lord about what to do. God answered his prayers and told him what to pay for the farm. This started Byrd's dream of owning a dairy farm.

Byrd and Mary Ellen's life was centered around the church, family, and their farm. They were very faithful to the Oregonia Church of God. They never missed a service unless it was raining, since neither of them drove. Whenever there was a revival or event at the church, they would finish their milking and chores early. They did all this without electricity and used kerosene lanterns instead. Then they walked to church. They wanted to be the first ones there. Byrd didn't think he had a good service unless he had a good shout. His face would shine and he would say, "I feel like I'm sixteen again. How about that."

I don't know much about my grandmother Mary Ellen except that she was a wonderful baker. She fed all the preachers that came to visit and seemed to delight in doing so. She was educated and an astute businesswoman. She went to a girls' boarding school in Berea, Kentucky. She took care of the business part of running the dairy farm and the rest of the family's endeavors while Byrd did the farming and prayed about all the family's decisions.

The Lord blessed the Powells, and they became very successful in everything they did. It didn't hurt that there was plenty of children to help on the farm. Miley was the oldest boy. Then came their daughter Parrot, followed by Erby and Malcolm who everyone called Mack. Boys Arra and Nolie were next. Finally another girl, Geneva, joined the family and then their baby, 'little Fritz'.

Trust in the Lord with all thine heart; and lean not unto thine own understanding. In all thy ways acknowledge him, and he will direct thy paths.
-Proverbs 3:5-6

Marjorie with her grandpa Byrd Powell. Picture taken at her dad Erby Powell's house along the Little Miami River.

***

My mother's parents, Charles Reeves Steffy and Cora Steffy, lived in Dayton Ohio. All their children were born in Dayton except for Monta. She was Charles' child from his first marriage to Alma. Alma had died from tuberculosis when Monta was just a baby. Cora was Alma's sister and Charles's second wife.

Dayton was a growing city in those days with many attractions. The Steffy children looked forward to Saturdays when they got to go to the movies after they had finished their chores.

On the way to the theater, they walked past a little church called the First Church of God. Mary, my mother, heard the music and singing inside the church and was very intrigued by it. Mary convinced the others to let her stay at the church while they went to the movie and pick her up after the movie was over. She would give her money for the movie to the other kids, and then she would slip into the back of the church and listen to the preaching.

The Lord began to draw Mary in a mighty way. She could hardly wait until the next Saturday service to hear more about Jesus. She felt such love there. It didn't take long to realize she wanted what the people inside the church had.

One evening while the other kids were watching a movie, Mary gave her heart to the Lord. She loved the Lord. She wanted to know more about the Jesus they sang and talked about at that little church. At home she wanted to pray at Papa's feet before going to bed each night. But she didn't have anyone in the family to teach her where to go from there.

God saw her hungry heart and would use her in ways she never dreamed of. There were exciting days to come for Mary Steffy.

> *For God so loved the world, that he gave his only begotten Son, that whosoever believeth on him should not perish, but have everlasting life.* -John 3:16

***

In 1925 Grandpa Steffy purchased a home for his family on top of Emmons Hill in Oregonia. Whenever a family moved into the community, especially a large family with several pretty daughters, everyone was interested in meeting them.

By this time there was Monta, Katherine, Mary, James, Florence, Charles, Herbert, and Frank in the family. There was a big steel bridge that spanned the Little Miami River in Oregonia where the neighborhood boys sat so they could get a good look at the Steffy girls as they moved in.

Erby Powell was one of those boys. As soon as he saw Mary, he pointed to her and said, "She's mine!"

She was the prettiest girl of the bunch with long beautiful, dark brown hair and blue-green eyes. Erby wasn't one to back down from a challenge. Once he made his mind up, he set about trying to win Mary's heart. He would follow her home from school trying to get acquainted with her. It wasn't easy because Mary was so shy, but finally he succeeded.

Planning for the wedding began. Excitement was in the air. Mary's Grandma Steffy wanted to create a special wedding dress for the beautiful bride. She used expensive soft blue silk and covered the buttons with the same material. She worked on the dress from her wheelchair and sometimes even from her bed. She was anxious to finish in time for the wedding. The dress was one-of-a-kind. This designer dress was designed especially for Mary by her grandmother.

Mary Elizabeth Steffy and Erby Powell. United in marriage December 12, 1926.

Mary, whom the family called Molly when she was young, married Erby Powell on December 12, 1926. Mary was nervous. She was only sixteen and her groom was twenty-one. In the beginning, neither the Powells nor the Steffys were happy about the marriage because Mary was so young. But Erby was determined to win them over, and he did.

That morning Mary slipped into the soft silk dress her grandmother had so lovingly created, and a unique necklace was placed around her neck. Erby was a handsome groom with blue eyes and wavy brown hair. Though Mary didn't know it at the time, he was quite nervous too. He couldn't even remember how to tie the necktie he planned to wear. Was it over or under or around? His fumbling and confusion over the tie caused him to arrive late to the courthouse in Lebanon, Ohio.

Regardless of the nerves of the two young people, the ceremony went smoothly. Erby placed a gold band on his bride's finger. Their vows were sealed with a kiss. Mary was a virtuous woman and wanted to be the best wife she could to her new husband. She treasured his ring and always kept it in a special place anytime she had to take it off while doing chores that might damage it. Much to her dismay, the ring was stolen years later when she and Erby were out of the house. They never found out what happened to it. Mary missed it to her last day.

One time years later after Mom had passed away, I asked Dad to tell me about Mom. He thought a minute and then said, "She was just a doll."

I've never forgotten that.

Who can find a virtuous woman? For her price is far above rubies. -Proverbs 31:10

I remember Mom telling me once I should never marry for pity's sake. I always wondered if she married Dad because he wore her down.

Mary was the third girl of the Steffy family. Growing up, Monta and Katherine always shooed her out of the house when they were cooking and cleaning. They believed it was easier to do the chores themselves than take the time to fool with teaching their little sister. So when Mom and Dad married she didn't know how to do even the most basic housekeeping chore. But Dad was so in love with her, he was patient with her bumbling attempts at cooking and cleaning.

Times were tough, and Dad had a hard time finding steady work. With nowhere else to go, he and Mom moved in with his parents. One day while Mom was lying down in the next room, she overheard Dad's mother Mary Ellen reading from a letter that had come for Dad. It was from a girl in Hamilton who had a son she claimed belonged to Dad. As Grandma read, it became apparent to Mom this was the woman Mary Ellen had wanted Dad to marry.

Mom was three months pregnant with her first baby at the time, and her heart was broken. She felt as if her world had been snatched out from under her as she crept up the stairs to get her things from the little room she shared with Dad. Where would she go? What would she do? How could Erby have done this to her and their baby?

Shame and embarrassment filled her heart. She hated confrontation. How could she face him or Grandma Powell? What if the young woman showed up with her baby? From the way Mary Ellen sounded while reading the letter, Mom wondered whose side she would take.

With no other options, and fear and betrayal in her heart, she walked nearly three miles to her parents' house. She was only seventeen. She was so young, newly married, expecting a baby, and away from home for the first time in her life. It was a lot for any young woman to process.

Mom continued to live with her parents. Dad came to visit often and pleaded with her to give him another chance. He promised he would rent a farm so they would have their own home. He found some furniture from a doctor who was retiring, and he planned to buy it for her.

Mom was such a gentle person. It was hard for her to stand up for herself. She tried to forget about the other woman and the baby out there somewhere. She prayed for God to help her be a good wife and mother. Fortunately she had a loving and understanding family to lean on during this trying time. She knew many young women in her position didn't have that.

She also had her faith. It gave her courage and strength to face what lay ahead. As her time for giving birth grew closer, she leaned on the Lord more and more. She would lie across her bed in the afternoons when she was tired and depressed and pour out her heart to the Lord. She begged him to tell her what to do.

She didn't want to make a move without the Lord's leading. She knew she couldn't trust her feelings to make the right decision.

Many times during her moments of despair and confusion, Mom prayed God would take her and her baby. It would be so much easier to just close her eyes and not wake up than to face an uncertain future with a baby and a man she didn't know if she could ever trust again.

But thanks be to God. He had big plans for Mom and her baby. While working as a seamstress in a private home, her employer had a child named Marjorie Jean who was a delight. Mom adored her. She loved the child and decided if her baby was a girl, she would name her Marjorie Jean.

CHAPTER TWO

On April 21, 1928, Dr. Ed Blair from Lebanon, Ohio came to the Steffy home and delivered Mom's baby. I've never been very big, but the night I came into the world, I weighed just a little over four pounds. The doctor told Mom I didn't have a high survival rate. I was anemic and very small. He said I wouldn't live to the age of twenty-one.

The next morning our doctor's brother delivered Katherine's baby, my first cousin Robert Dale Schuyler. He was a whopper. He weighed over ten pounds and was quite a contrast to little old me. Robert and I were the first grandchildren in the Steffy family. Grandma Steffy had to take care of us and Mom and Aunt Katherine. She often laughed about the differences in changing and bathing a ten-pound baby and a four-pound baby. She loved spending time with us and playing with us, and I'm sure we loved her even then.

I stayed close to my cousin Robert as we grew up. When he got older, his mother made him take piano lessons. He despised them as a boy but was happy as he got older that he knew how to play. He would play the piano, and we would sing the song, "*When you and I were young, Maggie.*" Nobody was allowed to call me Maggie but Robert. Everyone else called me Marjorie Jean.

Dad continued to woo Mom. He visited her at her parents' house nearly every evening after work. He adored me and played with me every time he came to the house. Oftentimes he would come straight from the fields to visit us. As he walked through the fields and across the backyard, he would sing Patty Cake and clap his hands. I would hear him coming and start bouncing up and down, squealing and clapping my hands in anticipation.

As I look back over my life, I know Dad loved me from the very beginning. He wasn't a demonstrative man and didn't know how to show his feelings. He never whipped me though he believed in it because he whipped my brothers a lot.

Mom continued to pray and seek the Lord over what she should do. She still didn't know if she could trust Dad. Her pain and sense of betrayal were strong, but she knew God was stronger. She wanted to do what was right for me. Mom believed since she and Dad had a child, they needed to reconcile. When I was about nine months old, she wrote a letter to Dad telling him she would come back to him. She carried the letter in her pocket for several weeks while praying about what to do. One day she felt led to finally put the letter into the post office box.

And we know that all things work together for good to them that love God, to them who are called according to his purpose. -Romans 8:28

Oregonia, 1928. Marjorie, 8 months.

*Marjorie with her aunt Katherine Schuyler.
Katherine was Marjorie's favorite aunt.*

***

Dad was a man of his word. He rented a farmhouse for us on the other end of Oregonia the way he promised Mom he would. He bought the furniture he found from the doctor who was retiring. The furniture was high quality, the best available at the time, and very beautiful. Some of the pieces had marble tops.

When I was very little, I loved playing in Mom and Dad's bedroom, I would jump on the bed as high as I could and look at the beautiful dresser. If I jumped high enough, I could see a little girl looking back at me from the dresser. I thought she was playing hide and seek with me.

I was so excited about having a playmate. I climbed off the bed and searched the whole room over for her, but I never found the little girl playing games with me. In frustration, I went and told Mother about her. She smiled lovingly and tried to explain I was only seeing my reflection in the mirror.

Mom's dresser was an extraordinary piece of furniture. A member of the family had seen it and fell in love with it. He kept asking Mom to sell it to him and continuously raised the price he was willing to pay. Mom finally relented and sold the dresser. I was sad that my little friend who played hide and seek with me was gone forever. It wasn't until later when I was sitting on the sink while Dad shaved and I saw my face in the mirror that I understood what Mom had been trying to tell me about my reflection and my friend in the mirror.

My Hometown

Much of the following information was gathered from the book, Oregonia History, by Kris Lewis, Oct 1995.

I loved growing up in Oregonia. It was a beautiful little town on the banks of the Little Miami River. Quaker families began to arrive in 1802 and '03 to carve out a community. Veterans of the American Revolution also settled in the area since they had been given land grants by the government for their service in the war. Salesmen sold land to pioneers from the East, sight unseen. Prisoners came from all over, too, to make a new start in this rough, untamed land. Of course, we can't forget the first settlers, the Native Americans who loved and hunted the land.

Hills rose up on either side of the Little Miami River, which were very steep, rugged, and wild. It was an ideal location for the mills that operated there throughout the years. Farmers had to work hard to earn a living since the land was difficult to cultivate. Some naturalists claim, that to their way of thinking, never in the history of mankind is there a greater variety of trees than in the Miami Valley.

During that early period, many settlements sprang up around the Carding Mill and Brown Mill. In 1816 a cotton factory moved to the area. A pottery, blacksmith, and sugar factory soon followed. The community used the name of Freeport. Not until 1845 when a post office was established, did the name of the town become a concern. According to the post office, there was already a town with the same name in eastern Ohio. The railroad had already arrived in Freeport, and they refused to accept a name change. Finally in 1882, a compromise was reached between the federal government and the railroad, and the town's name was changed to Oregonia.

In 1848, the Sherwood store was established by Jonathon Sherwood and his son Frank. The store carried groceries, clothing, footwear, yard goods, and hardware. The store was also the location of the Post Office. It was the hub of the community. Customers could trade eggs and butter for whatever they needed, pick up their mail, and learn all the latest news and gossip in one location. The store closed in 1943 after ninety-five years in operation.

A barrel factory was established and provided jobs for the town. Spencer and Monroe had one of the finest mills in the country, making and selling Acme flour. The company also sold coal, feed, and roofing supplies. The flourmill burned to the ground on Christmas Day, 1852 because of the careless use of firecrackers.

Bradburg and Spencer started another company that ultimately became known as the Oregonia Bridge Company. The Oregonia Bridge spanning the Little Miami River was an engineering marvel for its time. The bridge holds many memories for me, which I will reveal in the following pages.

Beginning in 1944, my cousin, Kate Hall, ran Hall's Market, one of the stores in Oregonia for many years. The cinderblock building that housed Kate's store and the Oregonia Post Office was jokingly called 'the Mall'. Kate said that it seemed like her clientele changed every five years. The first five years she was in business, most of her customers were old timers. They bought mostly bacon, flour, lard, and sugar.

The next five years she started seeing younger people come into the store. They bought frozen dinners, Pampers and the like. Over the next five years, she started seeing more customers who had moved out from the city. Party food and beer became big sellers. It didn't seem to her like her store ever closed. It felt like she was open continuously.

Kate knew her customers really well and knew where every one of them lived. Her market only had one bad year. It was the year when all three bridges spanning the river were out within the same year. That had a very negative impact on business.

The Oregonia school opened in 1846. It was a two-story building with one room upstairs and one room downstairs. Both my parents attended the school, as did my brother, Herbert, and I. One of my favorite memories of those early years in school was running across the railroad tracks to gather walnuts to eat during recess.

Harvesting ice on the Little Miami River was a big business in Oregonia. There were two icehouses on the north end of town where a stream ran down off the hills to the river. The railroad was on the east side with the river on the west, creating a three-sided parcel of land where the icehouses sat. The icehouse walls were about a foot thick. They were filled with sawdust for insulation. Long chutes were built from the river to the icehouses. Chunks of ice were grabbed by a johnny hook and pulled up the chute. After the river had frozen thick enough (approximately ten inches) for a horse to walk on it, the ice was marked and sawed into sizeable pieces for sale to the public.

My birthplace was a busy, exciting community because of its advantageous location. The river provided transportation and power for the mills. The trains followed the river and transported all sorts of goods for use and sale. I remember a sad time when a man was run over by a train and lost his legs. Did he give up? No! He gave his heart to the Lord and eventually started a clock shop on Madders Mill Road.

It is believed Abraham Lincoln passed through Oregonia and Warren County before he had been elected President. The train he was traveling on stopped in Oregonia for water before climbing the steep grades out of the valley. During the brief stop, Mrs. Lincoln was presented with a bouquet of flowers.

The people of Oregonia were God-fearing and established many denominations to suit the residents' needs. The Oregonia

Church of God had very humble beginnings. Adeline Brandenburg moved to Oregonia from Kentucky where she had taught school. She knew how to organize and lead people. She was Pentecostal and started having prayer meetings in homes of other believers. God blessed those prayer meetings and people were saved, sanctified, and filled with the Holy Ghost, according to Acts chapter two.

Oh, what wonderful times we had at those meetings! However, the congregation soon outgrew its space. The congregation began praying for God to open up a place to worship. There was a blacksmith shop where a man named Jason had a thriving business. I remember when our whole family rode in a horse drawn wagon. Dad would go to the blacksmith shop to get his horses shoed and broken plows repaired. A huge old tree covered the front entrance to the blacksmith shop. Farmers would park their buggies and wagons or tie their horses under the shade of that old tree while they visited the shop.

I remember watching Jason in his leather apron as he went about his work. He would hold a piece of iron over the fire until it was hot enough for him to work the metal into a horseshoe. After the horseshoe cooled, he would lift the horse's foot and drive the shoe into place with nails he had fashioned himself. I worried about the horses while he worked on them. I thought it sure must hurt to have a nail driven into your foot, though the horses didn't seem to mind. Dad said it didn't hurt them. I figured he knew.

Everyone at our prayer meetings kept praying and trying to raise money to buy and refurbish the blacksmith shop. Jason was getting old and ready to retire. My brother, Herbert, had a nickel he wanted to donate to the fund. There used to be a list of everyone who donated for the purchase of the blacksmith shop. I sure wish I had a copy of those early records now.

On October 2, 1940, Sister Goldie Wilkerson, the Brandenburgs, and my parents purchased the old blacksmith shop for the sum of one dollar! The ladies of the church went straight to work. What a job they must have had! But what happy cleaning as they cleaned and prepared their first place of worship.

On August 24, 1941, the church was finally set in order with nineteen charter members. Reverend Newton Crider was the first pastor.

***

Like his father before him, Dad wanted to farm. The Little Miami River flowed past the farm so there were always people fishing and coming by. Mom and Dad raised sorghum and other crops. Some of the Powells were still not very nice to Mom, but she never said a word. She didn't want to start anything. She was gentle and kind and didn't want to live in negativity. She always made the best of every situation.

A railroad went through Oregonia, and the farm where we lived sat near the tracks. Trains passed through our area every day. We could hear the cows onboard mooing as the train rumbled past the house. Herbert and I asked Mom why those cows were on the train. She said they were being shipped to Cincinnati to be made into hamburgers and different things for us to eat. This broke our hearts so we prayed every time a train went by with cows.

The trains made several stops as they traveled through Oregonia to deliver mail and supplies for the general store where we shopped. Herbert and I loved watching the trains go through town every day. Sometimes the Little Miami River would flood and overflow its banks and prevent the trains from getting through the high water.

Hobos who had been riding the train occasionally brought ice to our house in exchange for food. We had no electricity so Mom put the ice in our icebox. Sometimes she made us ice cream from the ice. What a treat!

On certain days, Mom and Dad went to the general store to barter their farm items for things we needed at home. We raised sheep in those days. Herbert and I loved the lambs, but we were accustomed to seeing them sold in order to buy things for the family. That was how many families were able to buy goods during the Depression.

Some ladies in town got together and decided Oregonia needed a bread man. They baked bread and cakes and cookies to trade to him for other items they couldn't make themselves. He, in turn, would sell their baked goods to others in the area. The bread man quickly became Herbert and my favorite person. One day he stopped in front of our house, and we ran to see all the goodies in the back of his truck. Our eyes got so large at the sight of all those cakes and pies and cookies.

Herbert started jumping up and down in excitement as he cried out, "Catch a lambie for a cookie."

He learned to barter at a very young age. Mom heard Herbert's offer. She bought us each a cookie so no lamb would have to be exchanged that day. We still laugh at that early memory.

Give us this day our daily bread. ~Matthew 6:11

During the Depression, there were a lot of desperate, hungry people making their way across the country. Most of them were friendly, honest people who had been caught up in circumstances beyond their control. But some of them were up to no good and were often looking for an easy target.

One time when I was around four-and-a-half-years-old, a hobo came to our door. I didn't think anything about it until I heard Mom raise her voice. That's when I knew there was a problem. Herbert and I ran to the door where she was. An aggressive looking man seemed to fill the entire doorway. Herbert and I hid behind Mom's apron and peeked out to see what would happen.

Mom always kept a rifle behind the front door. She had gotten to be as good a shot with a gun as Dad. The hobo started pushing his way through the door. Mom told him to stop and reached for the rifle. She cocked it and held it against her, ready to use it if she needed to. She wanted him to know she meant business and wasn't afraid to use the gun. As soon as he saw the rifle, he backed away and left. Herbert and I came out from behind her bib apron, so relieved it was over.

God had protected us. We never knew what became of that man. At the time, I was just happy he was gone. Sometimes I wonder what happened to him and what he had in mind when he tried to get inside our home.

Not long after that, another hobo came to our house and asked for food. Herbert and I remembered the last man who had come, and we were afraid. Mom knew we only had enough food in our house for supper, so she asked the Lord what to do.

The Lord told her, "Feed him." She told the man to sit on the front step while she fixed him something to eat. When she took it out to him, he thanked her.

We did not know how God would provide supper for us since Mom had given most of our food to the hobo, but she trusted God without question. She never doubted. I was always amazed at her utter and complete faith, regardless of the circumstances.

That evening a car pulled into our driveway. It was Mom's oldest sister, Monta, and her husband Alex. We didn't see them very often so an unannounced visit was unusual. Before we could get outside to talk to them, Aunt Monta and Uncle Alex started unloading food from their car. The United Brethren church where Uncle Alex was pastor, had hosted a special dinner. There was lots of food left over, and they felt led to bring it to us.

We were so amazed. It was like a dream. We knew Mom's prayers had been answered again. Soon our table was covered with delicious food. We certainly had a lot to be thankful for when we said the blessing over that meal. It was a God-sent meal we will never forget. Aunt Monta and Uncle Alex were so happy they had been able to bless us without them even realizing we needed it.

Trust in the Lord, and do good; so shalt thou dwell in the lands and verily thou shall be fed. -Psalm 37:3

***

One late fall afternoon a man came to hunt on the farm. The days were already growing shorter, and there was a hint of cooler temperatures in the air. We children were in the yard taking advantage of what could be our last opportunity to play outside. The man told Dad he was surprised I wasn't wearing pants. Dad told him I was a girl, and he wanted me to look like a girl. Only when I was picking berries or a similar chore was I allowed to wear pants.

I always liked to visit Grandma and Grandpa Steffy. Grandma baked bread two or three days a week. Their house always smelled so warm and inviting. To this day, when I smell freshly baked bread, I think of Grandma.

Everyone in the Steffy family was creative and artistic. Besides writing, I have always loved to express myself through painting and drawing. I like to think I inherited those traits from the Steffy side of the family. My great-grandfather Steffy was a gifted woodworker. He built a chest of drawers out of five different varieties of wood to give to my grandparents as a wedding gift.

When I was little, I slept in that chest in their bedroom anytime we stayed overnight. Because I was so small this became my special bed. I was able to sleep in one of the drawers until I was six. The cedar smell in the chest was so good and comforting. When our grandparents passed away, my cousin, Robert Schuyler, insisted I inherit the chest because I slept in it and it meant so much to me. When I'm gone, I plan to leave the chest to my daughter, Mary Owenna. She is very sentimental. I know the chest means as much to her as it always has to me.

Grandma Steffy made the most beautiful crocheted bedspreads with curtains to match. She created beautiful rose insets in each block. She had a lot of satisfied customers who would order items in different colors and styles for special occasions. Many a young bride received Grandma's handiwork as wedding gifts.

My grandpa Charles Steffy had a saloon in Dayton. He was known for his wines. He grew his own grapes and raspberries.

His cellar was off limits, and he didn't talk much in front of us kids about what he did down there. Grandpa made sure I got the first red raspberries of the season. It was a treat to get any of Grandpa's juice. This was his business, but I think he enjoyed spoiling me a little. Since I was the first grandchild and I lived with him and Grandma the first nine months of my life, I was always special to them, and they were special to me.

Grandpa owned one of the first Model T's in the area. He sold his wines to area saloons and clubs. He generally went alone to make his deliveries. For a time he had some competition from another man who lived close by. But Grandpa's wines were a better quality product, so he didn't have to worry about being run out of business.

After the children were married, my grandparents moved back to Dayton where Grandpa died. The Lord sent Mom to Grandpa while he was sick. She prayed with him and talked to him about his soul. I believe Grandpa gave his heart to the Lord after Mom left. On the way home from his funeral, we were all happy. We sang hymns all the way. It seemed like the Lord's presence was in the car with us. There is no way we could've been so happy if he had died lost. I dearly loved my grandparents.

After Grandpa Steffy died, Grandma Cora went to live with her daughter Katherine near Lebanon.

Likewise, I say unto you, there is joy in the presence of the angels of God over one sinner that repenteth.
-Luke 15:10

CHAPTER THREE

The person who had the greatest impact in my life was my mother. I've shared many stories about her throughout this book. Her life was dedicated fully to the Lord. God used her in many ways. Through praying for the sick and helping start the church in Oregonia, as well as using our home to pray for the needs of others, we saw her prayers answered time and time again.

Mom was such a special person. I wanted to be a genuine Christian just like her. She was so beautiful and tender and loving. She could always see the funny side of things, even when things weren't going so well.

An important part of our lives was devotions. Each night Mom would get out her Bible, and we kids would find a place to sit and listen while she read. I don't know how many Bibles she wore out while I was growing up. She read stories like Daniel in the lion's den and the three Hebrew children. She had such wisdom in finding a story that was exciting to my little brothers and captured their attention.

After she read, we would all find a place to pray. We would pour our hearts out to God. Sometimes one of the boys would get a little unruly (their prayers weren't going too high), and Mom would correct them immediately. She taught us that talking to God was serious business.

Mom always told us, "If you can't get to me, you can always get to God." She said we could pray to him just like we talked to anyone else. We prayed out loud like Mom did, truly believing God heard our prayers as well as we heard each other.

I always had to hold the baby during these times, and it seemed like there was always a baby. With one baby brother after another I couldn't wait until I had a little sister to hold and cuddle.

Therefore be imitators of God, as dear children.
-Ephesians 5:1

"Let your Love Grow in Me"
by Marjorie Reed

I know not what the future holds,
For each child of yours, you have a special mold.
I'm not able to see into the next hour of this day,
But I don't want to fail to thank you for each blessing you send our way.
Each trial and test you send is meant to make us strong.
Yet under the pressures sometimes we say, "Oh, Lord, how long?"
No matter what, oh, God, let your love grow in me.
I gave you my heart when I was a child of nearly eight.
More than anything I wanted you to lead me in the path that was narrow and straight.
I wanted to be a genuine Christian the rest of my life.
You poured your love into my heart!

If you abide in me, and my word abides in you, ye shall ask what ye will, and it shall be done unto you. -John 15:7

These things have I spoken unto you, that my joy might remain in you, and that your joy might be full. -John 15:11

***

One time when I was quite small, I remember a girl named Bernadine who was dying. She sent for Mom and the Brandenburgs to come and pray for her. The Lord showed my mother that if he healed Bernadine, she wouldn't serve him and she would die lost. Mom shared this revelation with Bernadine. Bernadine assured Mom she wanted to live. She looked at Mom and said so adamantly, "I would never go back on the Lord. Please pray for me."

Mom couldn't deny her request even though the Lord's word had been clear.

Unfortunately Bernadine fulfilled what God said she would do, and she died lost. Later I listened to Mom and others in the church talk about Bernadine's waywardness after God had been so merciful to her and let her live. This struck me so deeply. I couldn't get past it for a long time. It was all the proof I needed that God always knows best. He sees the future and we don't. Our ways are not his ways.

God taught me so many things through my mother's life. I could never write a book long enough to tell them all.

> *I cried by reason of mine affliction unto the Lord, and he heard me; out of the belly of hell cried I, and thou heardest my voice.* -Jonah 2:2

***

Many of my childhood memories are of my brother Herbert since we were the closest in age. Everyone said Mom spoiled Herbert. I don't know about that. She loved each of us, but maybe to some people it seemed like she spoiled Herbert because he was her first son.

One time when we were very young and still lived next to the creek, Herbert and I decided we would cook dinner for the family. Mom and Dad were working the fields that day. Herbert and I were supposed to keep our baby brother George on a blanket at the end of the planting row until Mom and Dad got back to where they had left us. Taking care of George wasn't enough to occupy us so we headed to the house to start dinner. We were getting hungry.

We remembered Mom would fix cocoa by putting sugar in a cup and stirring it. We filled every plate we could reach with cocoa and sugar. We realized the cocoa didn't look the way Mom had fixed it, so we decided maybe it must need a fire under it. We found some paper and started a fire in the cook stove. Our Aunt Verna and Uncle Herbert came in about that time and caught us before we could do any major damage. Mom came in shortly after and just threw up her hands. We were strictly forbidden to touch matches after that.

Herbert and I were very close growing up. We still are to this day. Herbert was very stubborn, but it was his determination that has carried him through his life and still is today.

Mom was patient and gentle—she had to be in order to raise nine boys. It wasn't often that she had to scold me. Maybe that's why I remember the only spanking she ever gave me.

I was about five-years-old at the time. Dad's brother Arra was on the other side of the Little Miami River plowing a field with his mules.

Herbert was adventuresome like most boys, so we decided to walk down to the river to see if we could get Uncle Arra's attention. We noticed a big grapevine hanging off a tree near the bank. Herbert decided to grab hold of the grapevine and swing out over the river to get to Uncle Arra.

We didn't see Mom anywhere, but she saw us and hurried as fast as she could to get to us before we could do anything drastic. She gave me a whipping, and that was enough for me.

Since Herbert was so stubborn, every time she whipped him, he sat down on the ground and said, "Didn't hurt." So she'd give him some more until he finally decided it did hurt, and he agreed not to do anything so foolhardy again.

Children, obey your parents in the Lord: for this is right. -Ephesians 6:1

***

Herbert and I never fought or argued like most siblings do. We knew how the other one felt, and anytime we had a difference of opinion, we just let it go. He still says we broke the Guinness Book of World Records for not quarreling or fighting.

Regardless of how well Herbert and I got along, as our home filled with brothers, there were bound to be some clashes. I remember one time in particular when the boys really got the better of me.

Mom and some of my aunts had gone berry picking, leaving us children in the yard to play. I got into an argument with George over something, and sat on the ground pouting. Herbert and George slipped up behind me and put an old round washtub over me. Then they piled on top of the washtub and wouldn't let me out.

Even though I was petite, believe me, it was hot and dark and cramped inside that washtub. Yelling and kicking and threatening wouldn't get me out of there so I had to use my head. The boys wanted me to get over whatever I was mad about. They assured me if I wouldn't retaliate or hurt them, they would let me out from under the tub. Finally I promised I wouldn't tell on them or hurt them, and I would forget about the argument. They got off the tub and let me out. I was dripping with sweat, but I was free. That's all that mattered.

I was sick for the rest of the day from being under the washtub. To this day, I can't remember what we were fighting about, but I sure remember the way they got back at me.

For thou, Lord, are good, and ready to forgive; and plenteous in mercy unto all them that call upon thee. -Psalm 86:5

***

I'm so thankful for my Christian upbringing. I've experienced so many wonderful things because of it. I remember when Morgan and Adeline Brandenburg moved with their family from Kentucky to Oregonia. They were the ones who helped start the first Church of God in Oregonia.

My Encounters with Angels

Years later, two of Mom's brothers, Herbert and Frank, married Verna and Maxine Brandenburg, the daughters of Morgan and Adeline. Uncle Herbert was sort of bashful, but he was distinguished and proper. He really loved Verna. One time when they were still courting, they were sitting on a porch in a swing. A little garter snake crawled up Uncle Herbert's pant leg. He didn't know what to do. Verna got up and went inside to get him a glass of buttermilk. Now Herbert had two problems. Not only did he have a snake in his pants, his beloved Verna had gone to get him the one thing he hated to drink—buttermilk.

As soon as she was out of sight, he jumped up and tried to shake the snake out of his pants. He jumped and stomped, but that snake seemed to fasten on even tighter. Uncle Herbert didn't want to look foolish, but he was desperate to get rid of that snake, while hopefully not getting rid of his pants. Just as he heard Verna coming back through the house with a glass of that dreadful buttermilk, he was able to shake the snake out of his pants.

Verna had no idea what poor Herbert had already been through. He took the glass and smiled his thanks only because love makes you do things you wouldn't ordinarily do. He hurriedly drank down the buttermilk, trying to ignore how terrible it tasted. Almost immediately, he excused himself to find a place to get rid of the buttermilk that was already churning in his stomach.

He never forgot that date. He knew right then it had to be true love to go through so much for his future bride.

Another memory involved my brother George. Someone had given me a nickel. I never had money of my own. I felt so rich. I carefully laid the nickel on a kitchen chair so I could put on my coat to go to school. When I looked for the nickel, it wasn't there. I looked under the table, around the chair legs, and even along the walls for as long as I could before Mom chased me out the door to school.

When I got home that day, Mom told me she had found the nickel in George's diaper. I was surprised he could swallow a nickel. But I sure didn't want it after that. I couldn't touch that dirty nickel after the places it had been.

Mom told the story to Sister Brandenburg, and the nickel was donated to the church. To this day George's name is on record somewhere that he donated a nickel to the church.

My third brother Elisha was born in Oregonia. I thought he was the prettiest baby so far. When he was just a boy, he got in with the wrong crowd and there were a lot of heartaches, but I'll always love and pray for him daily.

CHAPTER FOUR

For a while Mom and Dad rented a farm near Harveysburg, Ohio. The house was originally a log house. Someone had added a large room onto the back of it. There was a pitcher pump in the log part of the house with a long fireplace that ran the width of the house. Mom cooked many delicious meals on that fireplace hearth. A ladder at the end of the room led upstairs to the boys' bedroom. Mom, Herbert, and I took clay out of the creek that ran through our property to patch up cracks between the logs to help keep the heat in and the cold out. Regardless of our efforts, the snow still managed to find a crack or two! In the wintertime we often woke up to find snow on our covers.

Mom ordered my first store bought outfit in April the year I turned eight. It was a special gift for Easter and my birthday. I couldn't wait to see it. The dress was a sailor suit with blue stitching and blue shoes to match. I begged Mom to let me wear it to school.

That day didn't go the way I planned at all. I was so excited about wearing my new outfit that I let the water in the wash pan for my bath come to a boil. I tried to take it off the stove with a dishtowel, but I wasn't tall enough to get a good hold on it. I tilted the pan over on me. The boiling water scalded my legs and feet.

Mom heard me screaming from the horrible and unrelenting pain and came running into the room to see what had happened. I was scalded so badly that when she took off my new blue shoes, my skin came off with them. Mom wrapped me in a blanket and scooped me up as carefully as she could to carry me to the car. My brothers followed us out the door, crying and praying for me.

With the boys watching from the porch, Mom loaded me into the car and we started to Sister Brandenburg's house.

I hurt so badly I thought for sure I was going to die. It occurred to me I wasn't saved. I believe that was when I came to the age of accountability. I started praying for God to save me. I wanted to go to heaven.

The Spirit of the Lord came down in the car and saved me, sanctified me, and filled me with the Holy Ghost. It even took the pain away all at the same time. When Mom got us to the Brandenburg's home, I couldn't speak English. She and Sister Brandenburg were shocked. I don't think they realized a child as young as I was could receive the baptism of the Holy Ghost.

I was so happy. I knew I had something I'd never experienced before. There was no need for them to pray more for me at this point because God had already done the work. Mom turned the car around and we went back home.

My little brothers could not figure out what had happened to me. As soon as I got in the house, I hugged them and smothered them with kisses. I loved them like I had never loved them before.

The blisters remained for several days, but there was never another moment of pain. One night I turned over in my sleep and burst some of the blisters. Still there was no pain. It was an incredible miracle.

I finally got to wear my sailor outfit to school. I was so happy and so thankful to God for all he had done for me.

About that time they began teaching evolution at the Harveysburg school. Most of us students had been brought up in the Scriptures. We knew what the Word said about creation. I listened to the teacher talk because I knew to respect her, but she was wrong. I couldn't help but wonder if even she believed what she was saying.

Finally I couldn't stay quiet in my seat one more minute. Even though I was painfully shy and knew better than to show disrespect to a teacher, the Spirit of the Lord came upon me. I took a deep breath and stood up.

"But the Bible says God created the earth, man and woman!"

I looked around the room in horror as I realized what I had done. I didn't know what would happen next. I felt like my knees were knocking together and my heart was beating so loudly everyone in the room would hear it. As expected, all the other kids were staring at me. I think they were more in shock that I stood up and said anything rather than over what I said.

Don't you know several students chimed in and agreed with me? I was so happy I had obeyed God.

Instead of getting mad, the teacher ducked her head and gave me a little smile. "I have to teach what's in the book," she said. "But you children are free to believe whatever you want."

This was my first witness at school. It was also the first time I recognized God's voice. The Lord blessed me in a special way because I chose to be obedient.

I'm so glad I learned to obey the voice of the Lord while I was a child. It saved me from being scarred by sin as I faced life.

In the beginning God created the heaven and the earth. So God created man in his own image, in the image of God created he them; male and female created he them. –Genesis 1:1, 27

Log cabin painted by Marjorie J. Reed

The Snake

My mother always told us kids if ever we got in a situation where we couldn't get hold of her, we could call on Jesus and he would help us. One day my girlfriend Jean Wilkerson came to spend the day with me. It had just rained and there were puddles all over our yard. Some were deeper than others. My brothers had gone up the creek to play. Mom said after Jean and I finished the dishes, we could go too.

Jean put on her tennis shoes. I decided I would go barefoot. I teased her about wearing tennis shoes. It was so much fun to splash in the puddles, and you couldn't do that with shoes on. To prove my point I stepped into a really deep puddle that was clear. I felt something move under my foot. I wanted to see what I had stepped on so I started to step out of the puddle.

To my horror it was a snake with little ones. The mama snake wound herself around my right leg. I remembered how my mother told me if I couldn't get hold of her, I could always get hold of Jesus. I couldn't take my eyes off that snake. Fear welled up inside me, and I was about to give in to panic. I knew if I did, the snake would bite me.

I had to do something. I cried out to the Lord with all my heart and asked him to help me. At that moment, I realized if I reached down very carefully, I could grab the snake right behind its head. God heard my prayer and I was able to take hold of the snake. I got out of the puddle holding the snake. I held the snake out away from me and hurried as fast as I dared to the creek. I threw it out over the water as far as I could. Jean and I walked up the bank to where the boys were. By the time we got there, I was so weak from nerves I couldn't play with the other kids. I just watched them from the bank and thanked God he was with me and he had answered my prayer.

Years later when I was working in my kitchen one day, the Lord spoke to me and said, "Don't you remember, the snake did not bite you?"

I knew immediately what he was referring to. A snake's natural instinct is to strike first. Usually when a mother snake is with her young, she is even more aggressive than usual. Yet she didn't strike me. She didn't even try. God kept his hand of protection over me.

I was blessed beyond measure with a Godly mother who taught me to always call on God first.

For every mother reading this, it is so important to train your child at an early age to call on God if they have a problem of any kind, and God will hear them. Teach them of God's love and protection. Sing with them little songs like *Jesus Loves Me* and so forth. Tell them stories from the Bible that illustrate God's provision and grace to those who love him. Your children will always know to rely on God for all their needs.

***

When I was a little girl, the Lord protected Herbert and me from something much more evil and frightening than a snake. Even now, all these decades later, it is difficult for me to remember this episode of my life, much less write about it.

I sought the Lord and thought long and hard about including the following story in this book. You'll never know how hard it is for me to relive that time in my life unless you've been through a similar situation. After much prayer, I believe the Lord has instructed me to include it. By doing so, I might help another child facing the same thing, or empower a young person who is the victim of abuse as I was.

During World War II there weren't many men around to do the manual labor on a farm that required a strong back. Those who were could easily find work from local farmers if they wanted it. The farmers had plenty of chores but little money to pay for labor. Most of the men worked for room and board until they felt compelled to move on by whatever forces drove them.

I was about seven-years-old when a particular man approached my father, looking for work. Out of respect for the man's family, I won't use his name in this book. Dad was shearing sheep at the time and needed the extra pair of hands. Dad did the shearing while Mom provided first aid for the sheep when there were accidents. She was relieved for the help as well.

Herbert and I were fascinated with the process of taking care of the sheep. We watched through the slats in the fence while our parents cut off the lambs' tails. We thought it was so cruel and wished there was another way for the lambs to lose their tails. Each time it happened, we would scream and shut our eyes, but we couldn't help but watch the next time.

The man Dad hired was good with the sheep. He was tall, or at least he seemed so to me at the time. The thing that stands out in my mind about him was his hands. They were the biggest hands I had ever seen. I couldn't take my eyes off them as he worked with the sheep. For some reason, his hands filled me with fear and dread. I thought it was because I felt bad for what the sheep were going through. It didn't take long for me to realize something much more ominous than that was fueling my fear.

Nearly a week after Mom and Dad hired the man, they went to a revival. In those days revivals often lasted well into the night. My brother George was still nursing so Mom got him ready to go with her and Dad to the revival. She knew it would probably be very late before they got home, and she didn't have time to get Herbert and me ready. Dad suggested she leave us with the handyman. He had been with the family for nearly a week and neither of them thought twice about leaving us with him.

I never questioned my parents, but I couldn't quiet the unease in my spirit every time I was around this man. That night Herbert and I tried to stay out of his way and played quietly in the living room. The man didn't say much. He just sat in a chair and watched us.

I kept looking toward the window and praying God would send Mom and Dad home early. The last time they went to a revival they didn't get home until after Herbert and I were asleep. I didn't want to go to bed that night with only the handyman in the house with us. I watched him out of the corner of my eye and grew more and more uneasy as I continued to pray for God to send Mom and Dad home.

Finally it was time for bed. Herbert and I went to our room and got ready for bed. Neither of us talked much. We didn't talk about the handyman, but I think he was on both our minds. We were just trying to stay quiet and not attract attention. The handyman seemed to sense our fear of him, and I believe he enjoyed it.

I climbed into my bed and pulled the blanket up over my head. I squeezed my eyes shut and prayed again for my mother. I wished she was with me. I didn't want to be alone with the man.

My heart plummeted when I heard footsteps coming toward the bedroom. It was him. What was he doing coming this way? He slept in the barn. Sometimes he even ate his meals there. He didn't belong in the rooms where we slept.

I sank deeper into the covers and tried to make myself as small as possible. "Please, God. Please, God. I want my mommy," I prayed over and over again. "Please send her home right now."

I listened to the footsteps as they reached my room. My heart was pounding a hundred miles an hour. Then the footsteps started my way. I was so scared I couldn't even think. I heard him stop outside my room. I wanted him to go back to the living room, but he didn't. After a pause that seemed to last forever, the man came into my room. I tried to lie perfectly still in hopes he wouldn't notice me, but I couldn't stop trembling all over with fear.

He sat down on the edge of my bed and pulled back the blanket. I tried to get away, but he was faster than me and so much stronger. He leaned over me and gave me that scary smile of his. Then his horrible evil hands started taking off my clothes.

I screamed as loud as I could while I continued praying for my mother. Herbert appeared out of nowhere and leaped on the man's back. Herbert was only five-years-old and probably weighed less than one of the lambs the man had been tending all week. He jerked his shoulders to try to get Herbert to let loose.

Herbert yelled and screamed in his ear and pounded on his head and back as hard as his little fists could. The man's face twisted with rage. His face was like that of an animal. He reminded me of an evil spirit.

He put his big calloused hands around my throat and started choking me as if Herbert was nothing more than a nuisance.

I couldn't make a sound, but in my mind I was screaming for God to help us. He did. If even a few more moments had lapsed, I don't think I would be here now. The man was choking me, and I was losing consciousness. I am sure if he had killed me, he would've killed Herbert next without thinking twice about it.

Suddenly the weight of his hands on my throat was gone. Over the pounding of blood in my ears, I heard my parents' car outside. It wasn't quite dark yet. I turned my face toward the window. The man must've realized I was preparing to scream for help.

He leaned in close to me. I felt his hot breath on my cheek. His voice and his words were so hideous. "If you ever tell your parents or anyone else what happened, I will kill you." He jerked his head around and glared at Herbert who was standing next to the bed. "Do you hear me? I'll kill you both."

Neither of us moved a muscle. We stared at him as he stood up and strode from the room as if nothing out of the ordinary had happened. We didn't move until we heard the backdoor slam shut behind him. I jumped up, and we ran to the front of the house as Mom and Dad came in with the baby.

Mom saw immediately we had been crying, but we tried to act like nothing was wrong. We didn't want the man to think we told on him. We stayed as close to Mom as we could the rest of the night. Herbert and I were too scared to talk about it with each other, and we didn't dare breathe a word to Mom or Dad.

The next morning the man was gone. No one ever talked directly to Herbert and me about what became of him, but we overheard enough from the adults to piece the story together. Someone in Dad's family heard that an inmate had escaped from prison somewhere in Kentucky. The man had been convicted of murdering his wife and his wife's mother. He had even murdered his own mother. Herbert and I couldn't believe it. Neighbors and other people in our area were raising questions about the man who had worked on our farm. He had appeared at the same time as the prison break and he fit the general description of the escaped convict.

A warden tracked him to our area where he was arrested and sent back to Kentucky. No one told us kids, but I believe he was arrested in or near our barn. As I listened to the adults discussing his crimes, I know he would've killed Herbert and me if God hadn't intervened and let Mom and Dad come home from the revival at just the right time before anything bad happened. It turned out Mom felt a need to come home that night, and they left the revival early. They had never done that before, and they never did it again.

Herbert and I never talked about our ordeal. We were too young to understand evil of that magnitude. We remained afraid of the man and his threats even though he was back in prison. Over the years any time the man's name was mentioned, I wanted to know where he was. It wasn't until I heard he had died in prison that I told the truth about what happened the night Mom and Dad went to the revival.

Even after all these years this is very hard for me to write. I only included it in my story in hopes of helping someone else who might be in a similar situation. Mothers need to teach their children confidence and strength through God's holy scriptures.

If I hadn't known to call on God that night, I believe that man would've murdered me and Herbert the way he did his own mother.

I don't believe there are many praying mothers left in the world like the one I had. My precious mother was a strong woman of faith who made such a positive impact on my life. Through instruction and example, she taught me to live a life of faith the way she did, and that's why I'm here today.

How will those mothers and fathers answer to God when asked why they didn't take their children to church and raise them in the love of Christ? I fear for those parents. The Bible says it's a scary thing to fall into the hands of the living God. We need to love and honor him and teach our children to do the same.

CHAPTER FIVE

Marjorie on the Oregonia bridge when she was 16. She was working at the Five & Dime Store in Lebanon, OH when this picture was taken.

y father Erby Powell was born in Kentucky in 1905. His father and the Powell family came to Ohio and settled in Oregonia. There was a school within walking distance where Dad attended. One time he had a disagreement with one of his teachers over his grades. That fight led to blows. Dad got so mad he quit school.

He was a very outdoorsy person. He loved fishing and hunting. When he was still quite small, he would go hunting alone. He didn't have a gun or a slingshot. Instead he used rocks. They were sufficient for Dad to kill rabbits, squirrels, and other small animals. He never came home empty handed. He knew how to follow moss that grew on the north side of the trees to help find his way through the woods.

Once Dad had a dream while he was seeking the Holy Ghost. In the dream he saw a large rock near a creek by the house. He told Mom about his dream. She believed it was of the Lord. She and Dad took Herbert and me, and we went down to the creek to find the rock. We all knelt down and prayed until God baptized Dad with the Holy Ghost. First he cried, and then he laughed as God filled him with the Holy Ghost. We didn't know whether to laugh with him or cry. We weren't used to seeing our father act like this. It sure changed our daddy.

There were always hunters or fishermen stopping to ask for permission to hunt or fish on our farm. Whenever they came, they would hand Dad a cigarette. One night Dad dreamed he was looking down the road and saw Jesus walking toward him. Jesus had a cigarette in his hand. He just looked at my father. It was the most terrible image Dad could imagine. From that day on, he never touched another cigarette.

He always told me, "If it doesn't look good for Jesus to do it, it's not good for us to do it either."

I loved my dad, but I had to love him from a distance. He was such a handsome man to me. I loved to comb his hair. When he came in from working in the fields he would be really tired. I would take a wash pan and wash his feet for him. I knew I was his favorite, though he didn't express his love for me very often.

My brothers and I always wanted to make him happy. He liked listening to boxing on the radio. The programs made my brothers even rowdier than they already were, if that was possible. We kept our couch catty cornered along the wall in the living room. We would have Dad sit in the middle of the couch while we acted out the matches we heard the commentators talking about on the radio. Dad would watch us and laugh with us. He always looked like he enjoyed it as much as we did.

Don't Ask Me

Coming from a large family of nine brothers, it seemed like problems of some kind or another were always cropping up. When Mom or Dad would ask, "Who did it?" I thought if I said, "Don't ask me?" I wouldn't be saying whether I did or didn't, thus keeping me out of trouble.

My strategy worked all right for a while. One morning as we headed out the door to the school bus, I ran ahead of my brothers. While I was hopping from one rock to the next down the lane, I heard the voice of the Lord. I was only about eleven at the time, but I knew the voice of the Lord when I heard it.

God said to me; "The next time your parents ask you who did something, don't ever again say, 'Don't ask me'. You simply answer whether you did or didn't do it."

That correction made me stop hopping. I continued slowly down the lane to where the school bus would pick us up, pondering the words of the Lord as I went. My face burned with shame. I purposed in my heart I would never again say the words, 'Don't ask me' to my parents.

I praise God for teaching me to walk in his ways when I was young. I'm thankful he helped me so I could later teach those same lessons to my children and plant some of those seeds God taught me into the hearts of my grandchildren and nephews and nieces.

Even a child is known by his doings, whether his work be pure, and whether it be right. -Genesis 1:1, 27

Jerry

When I was about twelve-years-old our family lived beside the Oregonia church. My uncle had killed a groundhog. There was a baby groundhog there, and he couldn't leave it behind. He brought the baby groundhog to me. It was so cute. I named it Jerry. It would stand on its hind legs and drink from a baby bottle. It loved tomatoes and would do all sorts of antics to get a tomato. I didn't know groundhogs were so smart and so easy to train.

My mother was expecting my brother James Arnold at the time. This posed a problem of what to do with Jerry after the baby came. She was concerned about having an undomesticated animal around while she nursed the baby. However, the Lord worked it out. We knew a couple from Middletown whose last name was Williams. They thought Jerry was so cute. They asked Mom and Dad if they could take him home. They took him to Middletown one day while I was at school.

Jerry became the hit of his new neighborhood. He would go up and down the street and climb the steps in front of each house. He would sit on the step and beg like a dog until someone came out and fed him.

Everyone thought he was amazing. Someone called the local paper and told them about Jerry. A reporter came and took pictures and wrote an article about him for the paper. Jerry became known as the Middletown Beggar. The Williams brought a copy of the paper out for us to see. I was proud.

I still missed Jerry, but my little brother had been born by then so he got most of my attention. Still, I'll always remember the Middletown Beggar.

Joseph Carrol

As was often the case in our household, Mom was expecting another baby. Little James was barely a year old, and Mom wasn't sure how she could manage with another little one so soon.

She was so overwhelmed by the thought of it, she decided to pray and seek the Lord about the situation. An angel came to her with a baby in its arms. Mom knew it was the baby she was carrying. The angel said, "When you sit at the Marriage Supper of the Lamb and look around the table at all your children who help make up the number, you will be so glad for this baby."

Mom wiped her tears away and thanked God for sending her the vision. After that, she began to look forward to this new little one.

I can't say I was as happy about it as Mom was. The first thing I asked after the baby was born was, "What is it?"

When they told me, I thought, "Oh no! Not another brother."

I didn't even want to look at him. Mom knew how disappointed I was. She was always so smart and discerning in these situations. Instead of lecturing me or shaming me about not caring for my own flesh and blood, she used her reverse psychology on me. She called me into the room and asked me to change his diaper.

I was still a little disappointed, but I couldn't keep from looking at him while I was changing him. I looked down at him and thought, "Well, he is awfully cute."

Mom could see my heart was beginning to thaw toward the new baby. Her plan had worked. "Marjorie Jean, I want you to name him," she said.

I was shocked. What an honor to name a new person God had brought into the world. I wanted him to have a special name. I decided on Joseph Carrol. Before that day was over, my new little brother had won my heart.

James and the Paint

When I was about thirteen, we lived on a farm. I had to cook for field hands. It was during the Depression and a lot of people were out of work. Mom had managed to get a job at Delco. Our family, like so many others, really needed the money. We were thankful, but that left me with all the responsibilities of taking care of the family and feeding our work hands.

James was about two at the time, and little Carrol was one year younger. I was supposed to watch over them while keeping up with my regular chores too. It was one of the hottest days of July. I had dressed Carrol in nothing but a diaper because of the heat. I was rushing around trying to get dinner ready and keep an eye on the boys at the same time.

I heard Carrol whimpering and realized the screen door was unlatched. He had crawled outside. A day or so earlier my brother Herbert had got a can of black paint somewhere and was working on the frame of an old bike. James found the paint. He got the brush and paint and went to work on the baby. Carrol was now missing his diaper, and James had painted him from head to toe with black paint.

Carrol hadn't seemed to mind the paint until it started running into his eyes. I couldn't even see his light brown hair from all that black paint. I prayed for God to show me what to do. I got some lard and greased him really good so his tender skin wouldn't blister. Then I fixed a tub of warm soapy water.

As mad as I was at James, I couldn't keep from laughing. Poor little Carrol kept slipping out of my hands. I laughed so hard tears streamed down my cheeks. Every time I started laughing again, Carrol would give me a dirty look as if to ask, "What's so funny?" James watched the whole time, wondering what all the fuss was about. It took over a month for all that paint to come out of Carrol's sandy blond hair. Needless to say, Dad's dinner was late that day.

New Neighbors

It seemed like every minute of the day my brothers thought up new ways to embarrass me.

One time we got new neighbors, and everyone in the family was anxious to meet them. They came over for a visit. The whole family gathered in the living room except for the two littlest boys, James & Carrol. I didn't really think about them not being with the rest of us until I heard a racket coming from my bedroom. I had no idea what it could be, but with a houseful of boys, you learn to ignore noise and confusion at every hour of the day unless someone is bleeding.

Mom had recently bought me my first bra. James put it on Carrol for a horse's bridle. They rode out into the living room in front of all of us...and the new neighbors. I couldn't believe it. Everyone thought it was so funny. They were laughing hysterically until they could barely catch their breath. I was mortified.

James and Carrol had the most fun of all. They liked attention, and the more they got of it, the more they whooped and rode around the room. They really entertained our company that night.

I'll never know how the evening ended. I ran to my room and hid there until everyone had gone home.

Risky Business

There was a creek that ran through our property. We kids loved playing in the water all summer long. Whenever it rained, the creek would get up pretty high on the banks. The boys would take lids from lard cans and anything else they could get their hands on that would float and see who could ride the waves the farthest.

There was a hill climb in Oregonia. Dad's brother, Fritz, owned the property and made lots of money from the hill climb. Long before Uncle Fritz turned the hill into a money making venture, we kids would take car hoods or whatever else we could and slide down the hill. I don't think our parents approved. But with nine boys, what could they do? The boys were proud of me because I was the only girl who would do it.

Dad bought a piece of property on the other side of the Little Miami River. Mom and Dad had to go to town and left me in charge of all the little ones. There were always little ones to be looked after. Dad had built a little camp house on the river. The boys were having a ball swinging on the grapevines over the steep hillside. Feeling a little brave, and maybe a whole lot foolish, I told one of the boys to open the screen door into the summer kitchen. I wanted to see if I could swing inside it from one of the grapevines.

I missed my aim and landed on the steps that led into the kitchen. I fell hard. I lay there for a minute trying to catch my breath. I realized I couldn't get up. The boys were really worried. They started praying for me. They got hold of the Lord, and he intervened. Before Mom and Dad got home, I was able to get up.

There was never a dull moment at our house. What one brother wouldn't think of, another one would.

Kites

I remember one very windy March day when my brother Elisha was about five. Mom had shown James and Carrol how to make a kite out of newspaper and attach a tail to it. They decided to go on the hill climb to see how well their kites worked.

From our kitchen window I could see them on top of the hill. They tied their kites to Elisha. The wind was so strong that day you could barely stand straight even without your brothers tying sails to you. Poor Elisha would go up and down in the wind. His little feet actually came off the ground. Dad yelled at James and Carrol to come back to the house. They did, but they left Elisha up there tied to the kites. The rest of us watched him go up and down in the wind until Dad made James and Carrol go back for him.

I never knew what my brothers would think up next. It's a miracle any of them are still here today.

James didn't stop getting into trouble after he grew up. I'll never forget the time he tried to master the art of roller skating. He had fallen in love with Lois Reed, John and my oldest daughter. Lois wanted to go roller skating and James agreed. The only problem was, he didn't know how to skate. So he went upstairs, strapped on his skates, and began to practice. All of a sudden the rest of the family heard a horrible crash. James ran into the wall and went right through the plaster. There was a James-sized dent in the room for a long time afterward.

Fortunately, Lois didn't hold his lack of skating ability against him, and they shared many happy memories together.

Growing Up

Like all brothers do, mine began growing up. Four of them; George, James, Johnny, and Tim enlisted in the Army. They thought it would be more exciting to go into the Army than stay on the farm. My brother George was our hero. He made a career out of the Army. He eventually became a First Sergeant. But he was a better soldier for the Lord than he ever was for the Army. Years after George did it, James enlisted and reached the rank of First Sergeant as well.

I am so proud all my brothers were able to graduate except for Edwin. He had a rheumatic heart. Even Herbert was able to graduate from a blind school. I just loved them all—all nine of them!

Tribute to my Little Sister Ruth Adeline

In the fall of 1939 my mother was expecting another baby. I longed for a sister, but Mom kept giving me brothers. Of course I loved each one of them, but I wished for someone to talk to and be chummy with. I was sure there was nothing like having a sister. I knew God always knew best about everything. I wanted to be submissive to his will and not complain, so I never said anything to anyone about hoping for a baby sister this time instead of another brother.

Even though I didn't say anything, Mom knew I wanted a sister. She probably did, too, though she never said as much. As her pregnancy progressed, she confided in me she believed this baby would be a girl. As in everything else, I figured Mom was right. For the first time, I let myself get a little excited about having a baby sister. Finally!

My dad's brother, Miley, and his family were going to the county fair. They invited Herbert and me to go with them. Neither of us had ever been to a fair, and we were very excited. Dad gave each of us a quarter to take with us. I was a little worried about Mom. I knew it was about time for the baby to come, and I didn't want to leave the house. Still, I pushed my worries aside and prepared for the fair.

Unfortunately the day didn't go as I hoped. From the beginning it seemed like everything went wrong. By the time we reached the fairgrounds, I had lost the money Dad gave me. Uncle Miley was impatient and getting aggravated with me for taking so long. The other kids helped me search my pockets and the car to try to find my quarter. We could tell Uncle Miley was mad.

I believe there must've been tension between him and Dad. Uncle Miley had several children, but he always seemed to want to be better than us as though there was a competition between him and Dad.

After I lost my money, he told me he was going to have Dad whip me when I got home for being so careless. I wasn't too worried about a whipping. Dad never whipped me. But I didn't want Uncle Miley to keep berating me about everything I did that day.

Finally the day was over. Uncle Miley was still fussing at me when we got home. I was upset and tired and just wanted to go to my room. However, as soon as I got inside the house I knew something was wrong. I forgot all about my disappointment over the fair.

While we were gone, Mom had delivered the baby. As she and I had hoped, it was a girl. The baby was beautiful, just like my mother with lovely dark hair that came down over her ears. Unfortunately she had been born breach. She came hip first, and her knee collapsed her lung in the birth canal. She had been unable to breathe and didn't survive.

Mom loved the name Ruth. She always said if she had another girl she would name her Ruth. The midwife was Adeline Brandenburg. Adeline had delivered all of Mom's babies so Mom gave her name to the baby for a middle name.

I felt like I had messed up that whole day. I wished I had been there for Mom when she needed me. I tried to keep my tears hidden for Mom's sake, but as usual she saw through my pain. She called me to her bedside and told me I could dress the baby however I wanted.

I counted it an honor. I wanted Ruth Adeline to look beautiful in her pretty white casket. I dressed her in pink and white, my favorite colors. Then I noticed how long her hair was. I combed it down over her perfect little ears with my fingers. She was so beautiful, and I loved her so much.

I knew God still loved me in spite of taking my little sister. He had a reason for everything he did. Ruth was a big baby, and Mom had hemorrhaged after the delivery. She was weak from the blood loss and was unable to go to the funeral. Dad took the boys and me. The funeral director or someone had brushed Ruth's hair off her ears, but she was still beautiful.

I couldn't hold back my tears any longer. I couldn't stop crying all through the service. Dad put his arms around me, and we cried together.

Dad didn't show us kids his love very often, but that day I felt closer to him than ever before. As the years went by, I never forgot Ruth Adeline and what a beautiful baby she was. I mourned for my sister, but I knew God was able to give me spiritual sisters. He would give me a true friend to be my little or my big sister.

I will be looking for Ruth in Heaven. I'm sure she's beautiful. Though I have missed her every day, I am thankful she never had to live through the heartaches of this world.

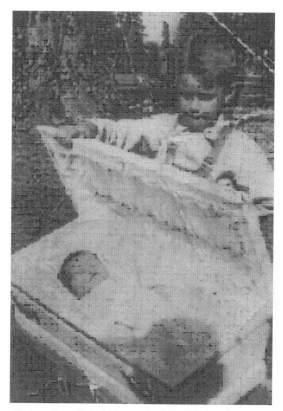

George Powell holding casket with little sister Ruth Adeline. September 23, 1939

CHAPTER SIX

Bible Training School

I was a farm girl and had never been out of Ohio. When I was fifteen-years-old, God moved on my mother to send me to Bible Training School (B.T.S.) in Sevierville, Tennessee. Sending me there would be a big sacrifice for her and Dad.

During the time I was getting ready to leave home, Dad was laid up in bed from an accident on the farm. He had been cutting wood when he fell out of a tree. A limb hit him on the way down and broke several of his ribs. The accident made it much harder for me to leave home since I knew Mom needed me more than ever. I hugged each of my brothers and told them goodbye, but I wasn't sure what to do about Dad. The Powells were a rough and tumble family. They weren't demonstrative and didn't say, 'I love you'.

Adelaline Brandenburg was the pastor of the Oregonia Church of God at the time. She and her husband were driving Jean Wilkerson, my best friend from home, and me to B.T.S. I started to go out to the car, but Dad called me into the room where he laid in bed. I stood there beside him, not sure of what I should say or do.

Dad took my hand and smiled. "I was afraid you would go on out to the car without saying anything to me."

I felt guilty because that's what I had planned to do.

"I'm going to miss you, Marjorie Jean," he continued. Before I could respond, he went on. "When I fell out of the tree,

I prayed for God to let me live long enough to take care of our family."

He cleared his throat. I knew he was having a hard time finding words for what he wanted to say. "I love you, little girl."

It was the first time I remember Dad saying he loved me. I blinked away my own tears and went out to the car where everyone was waiting. Before I got into the car, I turned to Mom. "I will prove myself to you."

I meant those words with all my heart.

This was a big turning point in my life. As the car pulled away, I couldn't bring myself to look back. I wanted to keep going forward for the Lord. There weren't many freeways or Interstates in those days, so it was a long trip to Sevierville. But we finally made it. In the beginning, I was in the girls' dorm with five other girls. One of them got homesick the very first night. The rest of us tried to comfort her. We knew she would regret it for the rest of her life if she went home without giving B.T.S. a try. She stayed a while longer but didn't last the first year.

It was great to be in a place with all girls and no brothers. Each girl had chores to do in the room, and it was to be kept spotless. We got demerits if we didn't keep things clean enough to meet the staff's standards. My job was dusting.

One morning our dorm mother came to examine our room. As usual she was wearing the white glove she used to check for dust. We held our breath during the examination, knowing she meant business and wouldn't cut us any slack. There was a large dresser in our room with a big mirror where all of us girls did our primping and powdering as we prepared for the day. The dorm mother seemed to have a GPS for dust and knew right where to go with her white glove. She walked purposefully to the dresser and swiped her finger across its seemingly clean surface. She turned to face us, holding up her gloved finger. I could see the dust on her glove from across the room. My heart sank. That dirty glove cost me five demerits. A lesson learned since girls do a lot of primping in front of a mirror. From then on, I made sure our room withstood the white glove test.

I had stepped into a world I never knew before. I was

Marjorie (on left) with her girlfriend Norma Jean Wilkerson at B.T.S. in Sevierville. Marjorie attended school there from 1945-1946.

getting acquainted with people from all over the world. One by one the girls began to thin out of our room as some went home or our housing arrangements changed.

One of the girls had a brother overseas in the Army who wanted to get mail. She asked if any of us girls would write to him. I did. It was nice getting mail from him and knowing I was making friends around the world.

My Calling

A revival broke out at B.T.S. One day I was sitting on my top bunk in the dorm room. God had allowed me to be alone that day. I had spent the day fasting and praying, wanting to know God's will for my life. I opened my Bible and my eyes fell upon Isaiah 60:1: *Arise, shine; for thy light is come, and the glory of the Lord is risen upon thee.*

I read through the next chapter. *The Spirit of the Lord God is upon me; because the Lord hath anointed me to preach good tidings unto the meek; he hath sent me to bind up the brokenhearted, to proclaim liberty to the captives, and the opening of the prison to them that are bound.*

After reading this, I knew without a doubt God had plans, and they were his plans for my life. God's presence covered me as I sat there on my bed in my dorm room. I had no doubt he was calling me to preach the gospel someday. I put the situation in God's hands. I wouldn't worry about when it would happen or how. I knew God had everything under control.

I told no one about my revelation. I just wanted God to direct my life completely in every way. I felt a little like I did when the Lord said I would write this book. It looked impossible for me to preach because I was so shy. Nevertheless, I wanted nothing more than to fulfill God's will for my life. And it happened just the way he assured me it would.

To this day I want his will more than anything else. That is why I believe it was so important for me to finish this book and be obedient to him.

In Tennessee, I met Sherman and Viola Cole, who became lifelong friends. Sherman worked at the atomic plant in Cleveland, Tennessee. He and Viola took in boarders from B.T.S. at their home. During my second year, Viola asked me to stay with them to help take care of their boardinghouse in exchange for room and board. I was so happy I was able to alleviate some of the financial burden on Mom and Dad. I had to do a lot of work for the Coles, but it gave me the opportunity to stay at school for another year.

Their oldest son Forrest was quite handsome, and the girls

swooned whenever he walked into the room. They thought he looked like Clark Gable. What a star. You could say he was my first boyfriend to a degree. I thought of him, though, more as a brother than in a romantic sense. I wouldn't let myself love him because I didn't believe he was the person God intended for me.

Forrest and I were always competitive. We loved to challenge each other in B.T.S. on who could make the best scores on our grades in class. Sometimes he won and sometimes I did. Other times our grades were so close we couldn't tell who was highest.

I'll always remember my last Christmas at Forrest's parents' home. I didn't have money to buy gifts for them, but Christmas was in our hearts and in the air. We knew what Christmas was truly about. Forrest got me a small gift. I knew it was from his heart. I carefully opened it. What a surprise. It was a lovely pin of two frogs chained together. I kept it for years though I didn't wear it often.

***

The family really missed me at home. As much as I enjoyed being around other young women, for the first time in my life, I missed my little brothers. Not only did they miss my company, I knew it was hard on Mom not having me at home to help with them. But the Lord made it plain this was his plan for me so it worked out.

Years later, those I had known at B.T.S. became top officials within the Church of God organization. This made me so proud of them. I will always cherish my time there. B.T.S. was also home to some of the top singers within the Church of God. I felt so proud just to be part of the congregation listening to them each week.

Mom's weekly letters to me had stopped. I knew something was wrong. Eventually I got a letter from my cousin, Arnold, who explained that he, a friend, and my brother, Herbert, had gone squirrel hunting. A terrible tragedy occurred that explained why Mom had stopped writing.

My dear brother, Herbert, had been shot in the head and

chest with a shotgun. Herbert had climbed into a tree to scare the squirrels down. He ended up falling out of the tree, and his gun went off. The buckshot caught him in the head and chest.

The boys thought he was dead so they hurried home to get help. When they got back to the scene, Herbert was still lying on the ground where they had left him. Dad ran to Herbert and picked him up. He thought for sure Herbert was dead, but Mom said she still saw life in him.

He was taken to the Children's Hospital in Cincinnati. One side of Herbert's brain had taken the brunt of the damage from the gunshot. The doctors told my parents Herbert would only live a half an hour or so. They packed him in ice to try to stop the bleeding so they could treat his injuries. The buckshot was scattered in his head and chest. If any of the buckshot moved from where it had lodged and went through the tissue covering the brain, Herbert would never wake up.

Mom never gave up hope. Her prayers prevailed. She stayed at Herbert's bedside for weeks praying and fasting. She sang and talked to him as if he knew she was there. Almost a month went by before he finally opened his eyes. His first word was, "Mom." That was the sweetest 'Mom' she ever heard.

Herbert wanted me to come home. Word got around at the dormitory and several came to pray about this situation. I was desperate to hear from God. As we prayed, the Spirit of the Lord came upon me like never before. One of the friends praying with me was a missionary. She heard me praying in tongues and told another friend I had spoken in perfect Chinese. God gave me assurance that he would spare Herbert's life.

School was almost out and we were having our finals, but I had to go home. I couldn't wait. This was more overwhelming for me than anyone could possibly know yet God took care of me.

At the bus station in Tennessee while I was waiting for the bus, a medium-sized man came over to where I was sitting. I had been praying and asking the Lord to help me know how to travel alone on my way home. I had never traveled like this before, and I was very nervous. The man was very polite. It's hard to describe our exchange except that he explained what I should do. There was a calm surrounding him, and his kind words soothed my nerves. He approached me silently and unhurried, and left the same way.

Hebrews 13:2 Be not forgetful to entertain strangers; for thereby some have entertained angels unaware.

I arrived in Lebanon, Ohio early in the morning. When I stepped off the bus, the heel came off my shoe. However, the worst thing was no one was there to meet me. I was disappointed and filled with worry for Herbert. But God used the situation to teach me to fully depend on him. I went into the Golden Lamb Restaurant and called my aunt and uncle to come get me. They came and took me home. Someone met me at the door and pulled me into his arms. It was Herbert. I didn't recognize my own brother. He was so swollen.

Over the next few years, pieces of shrapnel worked out of Herbert's chest, face, and through his hair.

***

After I came home from B.T.S., I knew I needed to find a job. Most of the young people who weren't fighting in the war found work at the local factories, businesses, and farms. In our area, most of us went to work at a canning factory. I made a lot of good friends while working there. It was work of course, but something I look back on fondly. While there, I met a girl who had a brother overseas named Bill. I was still writing to the brother of my friend at B.T.S., and we had developed a good friendship. I was eager to do it again with another soldier.

Bill was a great guy. We had a lot in common, and I looked forward to his letters. He was funny and interesting and was a believer, which was always the most important thing to me. We wrote about our hopes and dreams. Bill told me about his plans when he got home from England where he was stationed. I wrote about growing up with so many brothers and some of the funny things that happened at work. I even began to daydream about what life would be like if we fell in love and got married.

However, I always said I would never marry until the Lord let me know what man he intended me to marry. I was determined to be patient and wait upon God.

CHAPTER SEVEN

The year after I finished my schooling in Tennessee, there was a baptizing in Clarksville, Ohio. Reverend Jim Radar was baptizing converts. All of our family went that day. After everything was over, Brother and Sister Rader invited me to go with them to Sinking Springs where he planned to close out their revival the next night.

I had no way of knowing their invitation would change my life.

We had to stop at my house to get my things, so we were a little late getting there. Dottie and Manluff Reed were holding their service in a large room they had rented over Rhodes Grocery Store in Sinking Springs. We had to climb several steps to reach it. Church had already started by the time we arrived. Their music was different. They had no piano. A man was playing a mandolin, and a lady was strumming on a guitar. During the service, a little girl about two-years-old went to the front and laid her head in the man's lap. I figured the man was the little girl's daddy and the woman was his wife. Sister Rader had her accordion, and the Reeds invited her and Brother Rader to the front of the room to sing a song. As they began to sing, I felt the presence of the Lord in this group. It was a beautiful service.

I sat about halfway down the aisle on the left side of the room. I don't remember much about the service that night except I thought that sure was the cutest little girl in the man's lap.

At the close of the service, Dottie Reed asked everyone to come around the altar for a closing prayer. I went up with the others and knelt at the altar. I didn't know the lady playing the guitar was named Martha, and she would soon become my sister-in-law.

Years later she told me God spoke to her that night as I knelt at the altar and said, "That's the girl for John."

She passed the word to John. He told her that was just what he needed to hear in order to know what to do. Like me, he didn't want to make a move without knowing the Lord was in it. He knew Martha recognized the voice of the Lord when she heard it so it gave him a little push to talk to me.

Unbeknownst to me at the time, John was a widower. His wife Irene had passed away on December 31, 1946, a little over a year earlier when their second daughter, Leona, was only three-weeks-old. Irene had got up to fix breakfast one morning. John heard her collapse in the kitchen. He jumped up and ran into the kitchen. Irene was on the floor, nearly unconscious.

He picked her up and carried her to the bed. He laid her down and asked her if she wanted him to pray for her. She nodded and clasped her hands together. John prayed for her and got up.

"The girls are still asleep," he told her. "I'll go next door to call somebody."

Irene tightened her grip on his hand. "Don't leave me."

"I need to get help," John said.

Tears rolled down her cheeks. "Don't leave. Stay with me." She folded her hands and said, "Oh, Jesus. Oh, Jesus."

John sank back onto the bed. He took her hands between his and prayed with her until she slipped away at five a.m. and went home to be with the Lord. She left behind her husband, a two-year-old girl and a three-week-old baby.

In those days there was no way of knowing for sure what happened to Irene. There were no CAT scans or MRI's to find issues before they became a problem. Doctors attributed Irene's death to a coronary occlusion, but only the Lord knows what really happened.

After the church service over the grocery store, everyone introduced themselves to me, including John, the man with the mandolin. The Reeds lived up the street so we walked to their house. Brother and Sister Rader and I were to spend the night there. We all enjoyed a time of fellowship, and then we decided it was time for bed.

I had never slept in a featherbed before. All night long I felt like I was sinking into a hole with no bottom.

The next morning I tried to restore the bed to its previous condition before I had climbed into it. You were supposed to re-fluff the mattress to get rid of the valleys created from your body sinking into it during the night. I was small and couldn't master how to fluff it back into shape. Dottie Reed had to come in and fluff the feather tick mattress into shape for me. I decided right then, there would never be any featherbeds for me.

After breakfast, someone came by in a truck filled with peaches and stopped in front of the Reeds' house to see if they wanted to buy any. Sister Reed bought three bushels. I soon discovered she was a good organizer. She put Sister Rader to work washing jars. Brother Radar, John, and I started peeling the mountain of peaches while she fixed dinner. During the course of all that work, we got to know each other a little better.

John's mother told me later she could see the look in John's eye that day and knew he wouldn't quit until he won my heart.

A mother cat had some kittens in the barn, and two-year-old Lois wanted to show them to me. I told her we had to wait until we got the peaches peeled so she kept sticking her head around the kitchen door to see if we were finished. Every time she would look in at me, we would smile at each other. She was the cutest little girl I had ever seen.

When we finally finished with the peaches, Lois took me by the hand, and we walked down to the barn. She made sure I saw every one of those little kittens. Little did I know while she was holding my hand, that the next year she would be mine, and I would be peeling peaches for our family.

The Reeds had a large extended family. The cousins loved to come and spend time with Grandpa and Grandma Reed. During the visits, they would get out a rope and have the Reeds' dog jump the rope. Everyone loved to watch that dog jump rope. They would whoop and laugh the entire time until the dog was worn out. Some of the adults tried to jump, too, but they couldn't do it nearly as well as the dog. This was a fun time for everyone.

Once the Reeds got a visit from the Pollen family. Mr. Pollen was the Church of God State Youth Director. When everyone in the surrounding area heard the Pollens were coming for a visit, the Reeds got a lot of company. They wanted to visit with the Pollens, too, and hear him preach. The Pollens' had a little girl about Leona's age. I sat on the back porch and watched the little girls playing together. The Pollens' girl would pretend to turn a faucet and make noise like water coming out. Then Leona would go through the motions of pumping water from a hand pump. I couldn't help but smile. You could tell which girl was from the city and which one was from the country.

***

The Reeds invited our family to worship service, and we had a little gathering outside. We felt so at home with the Reeds and loved to worship with them. Looking back, I can see God's plan as my mother and John's mother got to know each other. Both were very dedicated and loved the Lord with all their hearts. God melded their hearts together as only he can do.

John mustered up his courage and asked Mom if he could take me home from church. She agreed. From then on, he ate Sunday dinner at our house every week. He even insisted on helping me with the dishes after we ate. That embarrassed me. I wasn't used to a man helping in the kitchen.

John Reed and Marjorie Reed while dating. Picture taken in front of Marjorie's parents' house in Elmville, OH.

Whenever John and I visited churches in the area, I always insisted that Herbert go with us. He was more than happy to oblige.

One night we were coming home from a fellowship meeting at a Pentecostal church in Beaver. Herbert had a girl there he liked. To get to where the cars were parked, we had to cross a small creek by walking on a log someone had put over the water. By this point, Herbert had lost about eighty percent of his vision. It was getting dark and hard for all of us to see, especially Herbert. About halfway across the log, we heard a loud splash. Herbert had slipped off the log and fallen into the creek. We worried for about half a second until we heard him splashing and laughing and carrying on. We had to fish him out and set him back on the log. By the time it was over we were all in a good mood.

The next time we went, Herbert borrowed Dad's truck. It had an enclosed bed and could hold more people. Herbert wasn't supposed to be driving since he was nearly completely legally blind, but he did anyway and drove wherever he wanted to go. There were about eight young people in the truck that night. I was riding with John in his car behind the truck. Suddenly the brakes locked on Dad's truck. Herbert mowed down seven fence posts before a telephone pole brought the truck to a stop.

We sat there a few minutes trying to figure out what to do when a man came along and saw our predicament. He helped get the truck back on the road again. We decided the wisest thing to do was go back home.

The next day Dad went to an auction and met the man who helped us get the truck back on the road. Needless to say, Dad was very unhappy when he got home. We never borrowed his truck again.

***

John's parents, Manluff Willington Reed and Sally Owenna Elliott, who everyone called Dottie. United in marriage October 31, 1910.

John Thomas Reed was born June 24, 1923 in Munroe, LA. He was delivered by a midwife who had recently given her life to the Lord. John's mother called him her little preacher man. She was a precious person who had a big impact on John's life.

John's father took care of a plantation, which was owned by his mother's brother. There were forty-some houses on the property for the Negros who worked the plantation. The family did business with the Hatfields from the Hatfield/McCoy feud. One time Mr. Hatfield sent John's uncle a bear cub by train. The cub didn't survive the trip. He preserved it and kept it in a jar on his desk for years.

Before John was born, his mother got saved at a prayer meeting. The next morning Dottie was in the kitchen doing her chores and seeking the Lord. While she was praying, she started speaking in tongues. She had never been taught anything about the baptism of the Holy Ghost with the evidence of speaking in tongues. All she knew was she couldn't understand a word she was saying. But it felt so good, she wanted to know more. She didn't know where to begin studying on the subject, and she didn't have anyone to explain it to her.

At that moment, she heard someone at the door. She didn't want to stop what she was doing to answer the door. She wanted to keep praying and find out what had happened to her.

The Lord spoke to her. "It's just as bad to act a lie as to tell one."

Dottie didn't know it at the time, but her answer was waiting on the other side of the door.

She went to the door with her Bible over her arm. A young blanket salesman stood at the door. He introduced himself as J.H. Walker. J.H. saw the Bible and said, "That's a mighty precious book you've got there on your arm."

Dottie wasn't sure what to say. She was still in shock over what had happened in the kitchen and was anxious to get back to it. But the young man was so nice and seemed like he might be able to answer her questions. She felt a little nervous about telling a complete stranger what had happened to her. But she didn't have anyone else to ask, and what did she have to lose?

She took a deep breath and told him everything that had happened, beginning with the prayer meeting last night. J.H. turned out to be just the person she needed to talk to. He told her he was a preacher and explained she had received the Holy Ghost. They talked more, and J.H. invited her to church.

Dottie knew without a doubt that meeting at the door was from God. Her life was never the same after that.

She continued to grow in her faith. She and Manluff were originally from Ohio and wanted to go back. They both believed God was calling them to take Pentecost to the people of their area in Ohio.

A lovely, God-fearing woman worked for the Reeds as a housekeeper. She saw to all the family's needs, especially those of the children. They loved her dearly and called her 'Mammy'. 'Mammy' loved the children in return, but she was especially close to John. Every Saturday, the family would go to town for shopping and to run errands. The older kids didn't want to go. They preferred to stay home with 'Mammy'. She captivated their imaginations with scary, spooky stories. The excitement and drama in her stories was much more interesting than anything they might see or hear in town.

When it came time for the family to go back to Ohio, 'Mammy' couldn't bear for them to leave. She said it was too hard to get so close to a little one the way she had with John, and then let him go, when she knew she would probably never see him again.

An old Negro man also worked for the family. He had never learned to read. Manluff discovered the owner of the general store had been overcharging this old man for years. Before Manluff and Dottie moved back to Ohio, Manluff paid off the old man's debt. He knew he could be prosecuted for doing it. However, he knew it was what God wanted him to do.

Manluff brought the family back before John started school. The Reeds were a farming family, and like most families of the time, they had a lot of children. Albert and Mary were the oldest. Then came Martha, John, Calvin, and finally Nina.

Dottie preached or testified everywhere she could. People knew she was genuine, but she still faced a lot of persecution for her faith. Over the years, she ran into J.H. Walker several times, the young man who sold her blankets and explained the baptism of the Holy Spirit to her.

My Encounters with Angels

Nina, the baby of the family, died when she was twelve from complications of sugar diabetes. She was a devout young girl with a heart for the lost. She didn't want anyone to do anything Jesus would disapprove of. She was very contentious.

During her last days, she got to where she couldn't swallow liquids. Her thirst made her very uncomfortable, but there was nothing anyone could do to ease her suffering. When she was dying at home, she said, "Oh, Mama. I see where the angels drink." After that she didn't ask for more water.

While John was growing up, he prayed for everyone and everything.

When John was about six-years-old, he had a pet chicken. The back porch had a loose board. One day while John's father was coming out of the house, he stepped on that board. The board came down on John's chicken's head and mashed it. John ran out and grabbed the chicken in his hands. He jumped off the porch and sat down in the yard. He began crying and praying for God to heal his pet chicken. His mother saw his despair. She went to the door and told him the little chicken was dead, and there was no need to pray for it now. But John wouldn't quit praying until God heard his cry. Suddenly he saw the little chicken move its leg. It jumped up and took off across the yard!

Dottie always said that was when God gave John his first miracle!

Later when he was about twelve, one of their cows had a calf that was crippled in both front legs. John's father was going to kill the calf because it was so badly crippled and could never survive. John begged his father to let him have the calf. John would sit on the ground next to the calf and rub its legs as he prayed for it. He wouldn't give up praying.

Again, God gave him a miracle and healed the calf's legs. This was his second miracle. His Grandpa Elliott made a wooden yoke and gave it to him and his brother, Calvin. It fit the calf perfectly. The boys would put the yoke on the calf and hook it up to a wagon. The children loved riding in the wagon with the calf pulling them. It was the hit of the neighborhood.

Everyone around knew God had healed the calf because of John's prayers. God was using John, even as a child.

John, his sisters, and Grandpa Elliot. The girl in the sled is Nina who died when she was twelve.

***

The first thing I noticed about John was his dedication. I had known other men, but he was the first one who really demonstrated his dedication to the Lord in his everyday life. I was so drawn to him. He was warm and considerate and loving. It wasn't long before I realized I was in love. I never knew I could love someone as completely as I loved John. I needed him, and he needed me. It was like God gave us to each other.

It didn't hurt that all my family thought the world of John.

The first time I introduced him to my grandfather Steffy, Grandpa said, "John, I want to tell you about Marjorie Jean. When she was a baby, she was so small we had to carry her on a pillow. Some nights she wouldn't shut up so I'd take her to the dining room table and dance her until she got tired."

That was his favorite story. He thought it was so funny. He told it to everyone.

John fell in love with the Steffys too. That meant a lot to me.

We hadn't been seeing each other very long when there was a special meeting at the Oregonia Church of God. John and Herbert wanted to go to the fellowship meeting and invited me to go with them. On the way home Herbert fell asleep. John seized the opportunity to ask me to marry him.

I was so shocked. I had no idea he had been thinking about asking me to marry him this soon. Before I could stop myself, I blurted out, "Are you kidding?" From the look on his face, I knew immediately he wasn't joking. I told him I had to pray about it before I could give him an answer.

As soon as I got home, I began thinking seriously about his proposal and praying about it. I wasn't going to lead him on if he wasn't the one God intended for me.

A few nights later as we were driving home from church alone, John told me he felt a calling on his life. He said he believed he would someday preach the gospel. As he was telling me this, I felt the spirit of the Lord witness to me. I didn't quite understand until I looked back on it. After I got home, I went up to the hayloft and prayed earnestly about this.

There was clarity when I prayed to marry John, but I needed further confirmation.

The next night Mom went to a revival in Blue Creek. I couldn't wait until she got home so I could talk to her about John. I knew she had a discerning spirit, and she would never lead me wrong. Finally the house was quiet so she and I could talk privately. I went into the kitchen where she was doing dishes.

"Mom," I said, "what do you think about John? Has the Lord showed you anything?"

She motioned for me to sit with her at the table. "Do you remember the time you asked me to pray for you about your calling?" she asked. "The Lord was very clear when he said he would give you a companion and you would carry the gospel from place to place. That day he said, 'Not now but later.' Do you remember that, Marjorie Jean?"

I nodded, anxious to hear more.

She covered my hand with hers and went on to tell me she had a vision about John before we ever met. She said the Lord showed her John and that he had two children. The first time she saw him at the Elmville church, she knew he was the one. She hadn't told me of her vision because she wanted me to find out for myself. I'm thankful she used her maternal wisdom to guide me.

***

On my twentieth birthday, John came over to visit. In his shirt pocket he carried a set of rings. He took my hand in his and slipped them on my finger. They fit perfectly as though they'd been made just for me. He asked me to sit on his lap. Then he asked me to marry him again.

I replied, "I reckon."

I don't think my answer was as romantic as he imagined it would be. I think he was worried I might back out. But since I knew he was the one, I never once doubted we would marry. For years afterward, John teased me about saying, "I reckon." He said it left him hanging.

John wanted to set the date that night. I took the calendar down from the wall. For some strange reason I wanted to get married in December, but John didn't want to wait that long. We chose June fourth, which was just a little over six weeks away.

Six weeks wasn't that long to plan a wedding so we needed to get started right away. John wrote to Brother Rader and told him he would have to finish what he started since he was the one who introduced us. Brother Rader wrote back that he would count it a privilege to perform the ceremony. The next morning when Mom got up, she asked why the calendar was on the couch. I told her everything. I knew she was pleased. The year was 1948.

Advice for single people who are seeking God's help in finding a mate.

For God to give you happiness, you must put him first. After that, he causes everything else to fall into the right category. You will have his approval on your life and everything else if you make him the most important thing. Both John and I put God first. If you want to be happy, put God first. He knows all about both of you, and he knows how to help in every situation if you allow him.

Our Wedding Day

John and Marjorie's wedding picture. June 4, 1948

John gave me four hundred dollars to spend on our wedding for a dress and so forth. My aunt Marie Powell drove Mom and me to town to shop. I wanted a new dress. It was Wednesday, and we had to hurry because the stores closed at noon. Aunt Marie took shortcuts and really put the pedal to the metal. We were off the seats as much as we were on them.

Our first stop was Litts' Department Store in Hillsboro. I saw a little blue and white linen suit I liked. I didn't see anything else I thought was appropriate for our wedding so I used twenty dollars of the money John gave me and bought the suit. Mom bought me a pair of white shoes and a few other things I needed. I was pleased with what I had. I went home happy and excited to finish preparing to become a bride.

I'll never forget the day before my wedding. I knew my life would never be the same again. I prayed for God to help me be a good wife. Since I would become an instant mother, I also wanted to be the best mommy I could be.

June fourth came. John arrived at the house early and sat in the living room waiting for me to get ready. When I walked into the room, his eyes lit up and he whistled at me. I knew I had his approval.

Mom hadn't told Dad we were getting married until the morning of our wedding. I guess she knew what he would say. And she was right. His first reaction was, "We can't let her get married. We need her too much."

After he realized the wedding was going to happen, regardless of how badly I was needed at home, Dad began to find other reasons for delays. He didn't have any razor blades so he had to go to Sinking Springs to get some. He was gone so long we began to wonder if he was ever coming back. Thanks be to God, Dad made it home with time to spare, and everything turned out okay.

Mom told me later Dad cried on the way home. I suspect she did too.

When we got to the minister's beautiful home in Oregonia where we would get married, they welcomed us in. They showed us a spot in front of a pretty bay window where the ceremony would take place. The sun shone brilliantly through the delicate lace curtains. I couldn't imagine a prettier setting for my wedding.

My heart pounded harder and harder the closer we got to the ceremony. My girlfriend, Doris Hill, and her little baby boy Howard were there to serve as witnesses.

It was finally time to begin the ceremony. After Brother Rader pronounced us man and wife, John and I just stood there and stared at each other. I think we were both waiting for the other to make the first move.

Finally Brother Rader said, "John, if you don't kiss her, I will!"

Everyone laughed, and our nerves disappeared. John kissed me, of course.

Meanwhile, the Radars two daughters put tin cans and wrote *Just Married* on John's car. We jingled and jangled with all those cans going down the road. John decided to pull over and take the cans off before we got too far. Both of us realized God had made our dreams come true and signed them with his approval.

When we arrived back at Mom and Dad's house where our friends and family had gathered, John came around the side of the car and scooped me into his arms to carry his happy bride into the house. As we came into the house I saw a beautiful double-layer wedding cake in the center of the table on a glistening white tablecloth. The icing on the cake was white, and it was covered with red roses. Mom had taken cake decorating classes by mail before the wedding. My cake was the first cake she ever decorated. I couldn't have asked for a prettier cake. Aunt Marie had baked it. It was orange chiffon.

Leona was only eighteen-months-old when we got married. She toddled up to the cake and swiped a rose off the side with her little finger. She stood there grinning and licking the icing off her fingers. I still couldn't believe she was my little girl. Then she dirtied her diaper. Thankfully John's mother came to the rescue. As I leaned over to pick Leona up to change her, Dottie took her out of my arms. "Not on your wedding day," she said. What a relief.

The neighbor boys came over to join the party and congratulate us. They brought a beautiful bouquet of live flowers. Those boys sure were hungry. Before I knew it the cake was gone and I didn't even get a piece!

John and Marjorie posing with their wedding cake.

CHAPTER EIGHT

First picture taken as a family in John's parents' front yard after Sunday School. Marjorie is holding Leona Grace. Lois Marilyn stands in front of John.

The Early Years

My brother George had been stationed overseas for years and had moved up through the ranks. Once he wrote home that he had been stationed in the same company as Bill, the young man I had been writing to at B.T.S. before I met John. Bill told George he wondered what happened to me over the last year since I stopped writing to him so abruptly.

I felt bad that I hadn't written to let Bill know I had met

John or about my exciting last year. But I didn't dwell on it too long. I was too busy in my role as new wife and mother to Lois and Leona to worry about it.

One night in 1950 after our daughter Mary was born, I couldn't sleep. I felt an urgency to pray for George. John was sleeping beside me so I woke him up to pray with me. I told him I saw tanks rolling over a bridge. At the time, George was a tank driver. Several months later, after he came home, I was curious to know if something had occurred on a bridge like it did in my vision. George said it had. He realized I was talking about a bombing that had occurred while his tank was under a bridge on May 25, 1950. That day happened to be George's birthday. He was the only one who survived the attack. God had spared his life again.

At the Highland County courthouse in Hillsboro, Ohio, there is a veterans' memorial with a brick engraved with George's name in honor of his military service.

George Ralph Powell

My Encounters with Angels

After our wedding, John and I moved in with John's parents until we were able to get our own apartment in Sinking Springs. This period with Manluff and Dottie also gave the girls time to get used to me as their new mommy.

Being a wife and instant mommy to two little girls was quite a change for me. I taught Lois and Leona songs they could sing in church. At this time we lived within walking distance of my parents. Every night we had family devotions just like my family did while I was growing up.

Sometimes John would read the Bible, and sometimes I would. Then the four of us would get down on our knees to pray. I wanted the girls to know when we prayed we were talking to God, and God was listening and hearing our prayers.

I soon became best friends with my new sister-in-law Armetha. She was married to John's brother, Calvin, who had also served in the military and fought for our country. Calvin and Armetha had recently gotten saved at John's and Curtis Robinson's first revival.

John and Calvin were working at the time at a power plant in Miamisburg.

One evening when it was almost time for the men to get home from work, Dottie mentioned Armetha and I should go pray since we hadn't got our prayer time in that day.

While Dottie finished supper, Armetha and I went up the hill to the old barn behind the house to pray. We climbed up into the hayloft. Armetha had been having problems with asking the Lord to fill her with the Holy Ghost. We began praying earnestly for God to baptize her.

As soon as she prayed, "Lord, fill me with the Holy Ghost," the Spirit of the Lord came down on her, and she fell backwards into the hay. Her head was hanging over the edge of the landing in the hayloft where we were praying.

I saw her fall backward, but I buried my face deeper into the hay so I wouldn't see her. It didn't take long. She came up speaking in tongues. The glory of the Lord filled that barn. It was amazing. We both began to shout in the hay.

We were so filled with the Spirit, we didn't notice when it

got dark. On the way home, we had to cross over several fences with barbed wire. We finally made it. At the house, they were wondering what was taking us so long. When Calvin opened the door, Armetha grabbed hold of him and hugged him as tight as she could. She tried to tell him she had received the Holy Ghost, but she was still speaking in tongues.

We were all so happy we couldn't eat our supper.

***

Later we found apartments in West Carrollton, Ohio, close to where John and Calvin worked. Armetha and I continued to grow close, like real sisters. I felt like I finally had the sister I had wanted so desperately when I was a girl. Every day we couldn't wait to get together to pray. We didn't care who heard us. We decided whenever we prayed, we would keep going till we heard from Heaven.

One day when we were in Armetha and Calvin's apartment, we really got hold of God. Armetha started singing in the spirit. It was so beautiful. We had broken all barriers.

When we came to ourselves and stopped praying, we noticed everything was as quiet as it could be. Someone knocked on the door. There stood some of Calvin and Armetha's neighbors who also lived in the building. One girl asked if she could come in. Of course we said yes. She told us her daddy was a preacher. God used this experience to stir something in her heart and draw her back to him.

Armetha and I were so excited to talk to her and listen to her story, we didn't even think to ask if we could pray for her. I always think back on that and wonder why we didn't. I think we were so shocked to see all those people outside our door it slipped our minds. After that day, we continued to pray God would deal with that young woman's heart. I'm sure he did, wherever she was.

***

I loved to tell John I really got a bargain when I married him. Each day with the two little girls was special. Lois always wanted to show off her new mommy, and I loved showing off my girls.

In West Carrollton, we had an upstairs apartment. I loved listening to the girls playing with the other children in the downstairs apartments. Lois decided one day to have church on the steps. She lined all of the kids from the downstairs apartments on the steps just like they were church pews. Her voice rang out loud and clear as she preached to them. I was sure all the mothers were listening.

Lois would tell the kids what they could and couldn't do and tried to prove it by me. Sometimes I had to ask God for wisdom to answer her questions. But we did our best, and God saved some of those mothers. Their children were so happy to report to Lois that their mommies were Christians now.

After one of their services, Lois came leading Leona up the steps to our apartment. She was very upset with Leona, and poor Leona just looked confused. Lois sat Leona down in a chair and said, "You stay up here till you get the Holy Ghost!" She was zealous for the Lord from the beginning.

***

It was always a special time watching the girls greet their daddy when he came home from work. They raced each other to be the first to see if he had anything left in his dinner bucket. While the girls looked inside the dinner bucket, John and I said our own hellos. One night I heard Lois say, "No, you won't smack me!"

Leona had her hand drawn back. When Lois said that, Leona smacked her.

It was time for Daddy to come on the scene. "No matter what happens you don't smack your sister."

I don't remember one of them smacking the other after that. When Daddy laid down the law, they kept it most of the time. I'm so thankful for the ready-made family God gave us. I wanted to be a good mommy and love them dearly, and I did. It was so wonderful to have little girls.

***

Raising girls was quite different from helping Mom take care of my rowdy brothers. Every day came with a new lesson for me. Our first Christmas together was the best one I remember. It was so much fun shopping for little girls for a change.

Not long before Christmas, John and I went shopping at the G.C. Murphy store in Hillsboro. On a high shelf I saw a metal dollhouse that would be perfect for Lois and Leona. I wasn't tall enough to see the top floor of the dollhouse. While I was stretching and straining to see, John came up behind me and picked me up so I could see. I squealed in surprise. I was a little embarrassed, too, especially after I saw other shoppers staring at us, trying to figure out what we were doing. I'm sure we made quite a pair, with me so small and John so tall.

Another time when John was running errands, he found a little washing machine made by the Duncan Company. It was a miniature model used by company salesmen to demonstrate the benefits of the full size machines. John talked the man into selling it to him. That little washing machine was the hit of our neighborhood. It had a handle on the side to crank, and the girls had a wonderful time playing with it. I set up a little clothesline, and the girls loved playing house and washing their doll clothes. The toy clothesline was always filled with doll clothes from every kid in the neighborhood.

The first year we were married, John worked for a farmer and a carpenter at different times to make extra money. He earned his carpentry credentials and got all kinds of good jobs around the area. It also came in handy when we were ready to build a church and our own house.

Not long after John and I married, Mom fell and broke her pelvis. She was expecting another baby at the time. John insisted I stay with her the last few months of her pregnancy to take care of her and Dad and the boys. John's mother Dottie kept Lois and Leona for us since Mom and Dad's house just wasn't big enough for all of us. John and I were living in Miamisburg at the time. John stayed there during the week so he could work and came home to Elmville on the weekends where I was staying with Mom and Dad.

Dad sold a calf that Mom had wanted to keep for the winter for beef. While I was changing her bed, Mom went to sit in a chair by the window to wait for me to finish. Her eyes filled with tears over the calf though there was nothing she could do about it now.

My two-year-old brother Edwin came into the room and saw her crying. He went over to where she was sitting and put his hands on her. He buried his face in her lap and prayed, "Dear Jeesy, do help my mommy!"

God heard that prayer right away. Mom had to chuckle through her tears. We all had to laugh.

Mom and Edwin, age 2, standing outside their house.

Dottie was a midwife, and it was arranged that she would help when the time came for Mom's delivery. The day Mom went into labor there was a terrible electrical storm. I never heard such a storm. The entire area lost power. On top of that,

Dad's truck wouldn't start so he couldn't go after John's mother.

Dad went out in the barn to find a lantern and kerosene lamp so we could see what we were doing. Earlier Mom had gotten scissors and thread ready when it came time to tie the baby's cord. That was one thing we didn't have to worry about as we fumbled around in the dark.

The storm continued raging throughout the day and wouldn't let up. Neither would Mom's labor. We finally faced the realization we would not be able to get anyone to assist in the delivery.

Mom turned to me. "Honey, it looks like it's up to you."

I had taken some basic home nursing courses while I was at B.T.S. so I knew a little about what to do. Unfortunately it wasn't much. I hadn't given birth to any babies of my own. I knew the basics of what to do during a delivery, but I had never been with anyone going through it.

I would have to rely on everything Mom told me. She instructed me to put some water in the big reservoir on the stove. Standing at the kitchen stove, I began to pray. "Lord, if you ever helped me, you've got to help me now."

I meant that prayer with all of my heart. God came to my rescue. His glorious presence came down and covered me from my head to my feet. It stayed on me till after the baby was born. I knew the Lord was guiding my hands and taking the stress away from me.

Believe it or not, that was the easiest delivery Mom ever had.

Years earlier, I had told Mom I preferred bald-headed babies. I thought they were just so kissable. When she saw the new baby, she grinned up at me.

"Marjorie, you must've wished this baby bald-headed."

All her babies had been born with a full head of hair except for this one.

Mom and Dad named the new baby Thomas Mark. There surely was something special about him. Maybe it was because God had performed such a miracle that day by showing me how to take care of Mom. Either way, after I washed and dressed

My Encounters with Angels

little Tommy, my strength left me. I got so weak I had to lie on the couch.

***

On August 2nd, 1950, John and I became parents together when our daughter Mary Owenna was born. We lived in Elmville at the time within walking distance of my parents' house. Mom was there for Mary's birth. She wrapped the baby in a blanket and laid her in my arms.

"She's just going to be beautiful," Mom said with such love on her face.

Baby Mary smiled, and I just fell in love with her. After Mom finished cleaning up the baby, she went into the kitchen to cook breakfast for the doctor and John. Dr. Cutwright knew John was a qualified and dependable carpenter. They started talking about some jobs the doctor needed done at his house. He asked John if he would build a chimney on the side of a house he owned in Bainbridge. He said John could do the job in exchange for delivering our baby. John agreed, and the deal was settled.

It was a beautiful time with a new baby and my family near me. Little did I know what would happen to our family just a few days after our Mary's birth.

When Mary was eight days old, a tragedy occurred that rocked our family to its core.

My brothers, James and Carrol, were six and seven-years-old that summer. One hot August afternoon just a few days after Mary was born, they went out to the barn to play. Always curious and exploring, they climbed up on some shelving and found the old lantern I had used the day Tommy was born when the storm had blown out the electricity.

Dad always kept a can of gasoline on a rafter in the barn to use for his power saw and other equipment. The boys got the can and the lantern down and decided to fill the lantern with the gas. They didn't realize gasoline and kerosene were two different things, and filling a lantern with gasoline could cause an explosion.

My brother, Tommy, was less than two-years-old, but he loved to follow his big brothers around and play with them. It was laundry day, and Mom had washed a lot of clothes. The line was full as always. With a house full of boys and babies, it seemed she never got ahead of the wash.

Johnny was the youngest at the time. At five-months-old, he needed Mom's constant attention. After Mom finished with the laundry, she decided to mop the kitchen floor really quick before starting dinner.

While the bigger boys were playing with the lantern and the can of gasoline, Tommy found a canvas seeder and started playing with it. One of the other boys slipped it over Tommy's head to keep him occupied and out of their way. The seeder was a canvas sling worn over one shoulder and outfitted with a crank the wearer would turn to release seed onto the ground as he walked along the rows.

Tommy stuck close to the older boys. They knelt on the ground to fill the lantern with gas. Wearing the seeder, Tommy leaned over them so he could see what they were doing. Inside the house, little Johnny was getting fussier by the minute. Mom had her hands full with all her household chores. While Johnny fussed to be picked up, Mom hurried to finish mopping the kitchen floor.

Earlier, while she had been busy, one of the boys came in and took some matches out of the kitchen without her knowing it. She was nearly through with her work and ready to give Johnny some much needed attention when a loud explosion rocked the August afternoon. Outside, the boys started screaming. Mom ran out the back door. To her horror, little Tommy was engulfed in a ball of flames. She couldn't even see him for the fire. The lantern had exploded, and the seeder had been ignited by the explosion. The heat fused it to his tiny body.

Mom tore off her apron as she ran across the yard and tried to smother the flames with her apron. There was really nothing she could do.

Dottie was at our house with me at the time. Someone ran over and told us what happened. We ran across the fields to Mom's house. Mom and all the brothers were hysterical.

Tommy only survived a few hours. When the coroner arrived to pronounce him dead, he told me, "You can only lose so much fluid in your body and still survive. It's like the body is bleeding to death."

***

It was hard to go home and enjoy my own little Mary knowing how much my dear mother was suffering. Mom had been carrying Johnny when I became pregnant with Mary. We talked often about how our children would grow up together. Our girls loved going to Mom's to play since they had so many uncles their own age to play with. Now everything was different. I didn't know if our hearts would ever mend.

The first time Mom came to visit us after losing Tommy, she looked like she had aged ten years. Leona Wylie was the wife of the man who owned the funeral home in Sinking Springs. She bought a handsome little outfit to put on Tommy for the funeral. I don't know if Mom couldn't afford it or if Mrs. Wylie just wanted to do something nice for our family. Either way, it was very much appreciated.

There was such an outpouring of love and support from the people in the community following the accident. It helped, but this was one of the hardest things our family had ever gone

Thomas Mark Powell, summer 1950.

through. A few days after the funeral while Mom was cleaning out the closet, she found the apron and sheet she had wrapped Tommy in while waiting for help to arrive.

***

After the tragedy, Mom couldn't sleep at night. All she could think of was her beloved little boy. The image of his body suffering in those flames haunted her day and night. One night after everyone else had settled down for the night, Mom got out of bed and went into the living room and lay down on the couch. Her pain was so great. She felt as if her heart was breaking. She didn't know how she would go on. She didn't know if she even wanted to. While she lay on the couch, all she could say was, "Jesus. Jesus. Jesus."

In the far corner of the room, she saw a light. She focused on the light and watched as it got closer and closer. The sight was strange to her, but she wasn't afraid. She continued to watch the light as it advanced across the room.

After a few moments, she realized the light was an angel. He landed not far from where she was on the couch. She saw the devil enter the room behind him. The light emanating from the angel began to wrestle with the devil. The devil was no match for the angel God had sent to protect her. Before her eyes, the angel and the devil wrestled on the living room floor. Mom couldn't tear her gaze away. She did not feel fear as she watched them. She knew the devil was defeated and had to go.

After the devil left the room, the angel turned his focus on Mom. He told her the devil had come to take her mind.

The angel said, "I've come to take your grief. The devil came to take your mind and make you ineffective in your purpose. But I will take your pain. You must not grieve for Tommy any longer."

Those were the hardest words Mom ever heard.

The angel told her one more thing. "You must set your mind on raising the children you have now."

Mom knew he was right. She still had a family that needed her. She knew where Tommy was. She could rest in knowing he was safe and at peace. Heaven had a greater pull for her than ever before.

***

Many years later in June 1961, my brother Joseph Carrol graduated from Sinking Springs High School. He had been working in timber and earned enough money to buy an old car. He had made friends with a boy from Germany named Peter. He was teaching Peter how to drive. One Saturday they were on a farm trying to get the car started so Peter could have his driving lesson.

After several attempts, they decided to use the truck to get the car rolling so they would have better luck turning the engine over. Carrol bent over in front of the car to hook it up to the truck. He wasn't paying attention and didn't realize the car was still in gear. The car began to roll and lodged Carrol's head between the car and the truck bed. The emblem of the car went through his head.

Peter ran to the house to get help. Carrol died at the hospital as they were taking him out of the car. This has been one of the hardest things in my life I've ever been through.

My mother had been ill when this happened. During the visitation and memorial service we kept her in the other room away from the casket so she could still receive condolences from friends and family without seeing Carrol.

So much love went out to her. Joseph Carrol was loved by many people, and everyone loved Mom.

Joseph Carrol Powell

After Joseph Carrol's death, I moved into the house with Mom and Dad for a while. I didn't want Mom to be alone. There was so much death and mourning. Over a two-year period, there was a total of twelve deaths in the family. It seemed like we couldn't get over one when another one would occur.

Several months before Carrol died, I had been praying for his salvation. He was a good kid, but I wanted to know he was ready to meet the Lord. I could tell he was struggling with holding onto his salvation. Every time I prayed for him, I could see him tossing and turning on his bed like the Lord was dealing with him.

Each time my vision was the same.

After Carrol's death, Mom and I wanted some kind of assurance from the Lord so we would know where his soul was. One night both of us had a dream. The next morning we could hardly wait to tell one another about our dream. It was amazing. As soon as we started talking, we realized we had the same dream!

In our dreams, we saw Joseph Carrol in heaven wearing a robe and marching in with a choir. He was so happy. The dreams wiped away any doubts Mom and I had of where he was. We were finally at peace and able to wipe our tears away.

Mom had to drink the cup of suffering many times through her life. There were times over the years she felt the urge to fall back into that pit of depression. She kept in mind the vision God had given her of the angel wrestling with the devil on her behalf, and she would rise above it.

The angel of the Lord encampeth round about them that fear him, and delivereth them. -Genesis 1:1, 27

CHAPTER NINE

Our Ministry Begins

Our first church, Blue Creek Church of God

While John was working hard to support us, he also got his license to enter the ministry. His mother and my mother had done a revival in Blue Creek, Ohio before John and I married, and the people from that congregation remembered him. They wrote to him and asked if he would consider becoming their minister.

On a cold March day in 1952, we moved into our first parsonage in Blue Creek. It was sleeting outside when we arrived. There was no electricity in the house. We brought a little wood king heater stove with us. John made the girls and me wait in the car until he got a fire going.

In order to fetch firewood for us, he had to climb a steep

bank behind our house. For our water supply, he had to carry two five-gallon buckets up the bank on the other side of the house and through a field to a spring. He sure did a lot of running back and forth while we lived in that parsonage.

We also had an old wood cook stove that helped heat the house. Sister Copas was our landlord. She was a lovely lady and didn't charge us any rent.

Lois was in the first grade when we moved to Blue Creek. She walked to the end of our road every morning to catch the school bus. Leona was four and a half and Mary was two. At this time we were living by faith. The only income we received was sixty dollars a month rent from my brother, Herbert, and his wife Ruth. There was an elderly lady that would take Lois to her house when it was cold. We appreciated that so much. This was quite an adventure for Lois to be in a new environment and meet new people.

John and I had lots to learn about leading a flock. Blue Creek will always have a soft spot in my heart. The congregation won our hearts, and I think we won theirs though it took some time. One time when we went back home to visit Mom, some of the teenage girls from the church came and cleaned our house. That really touched my heart.

On our way to Mom's house, we had to cross a set of railroad tracks. We would often meet the train. The conductor would wave to Mary, and she would wave back. There were so many little things that the church did for us. Separately they didn't seem to amount to much, but it sure meant a lot to us.

Early on in our relationship, John and I made a decision to give God first place in our lives. We trusted that everything else would fall into place if we did.

We wanted to be good pastors to the people of Blue Creek. God showed us favor and we loved those precious people with all our hearts. Both of us were in our twenties at the time with so much to learn. When we came up against a problem we didn't know how to solve, we prayed until God gave us the answer.

We learned a lot over the years while pastoring churches. Every individual is different and has been equipped with different strengths. God has a specific purpose for each one of us as we work to build his kingdom. It is the responsibility of every believer to discover that purpose for themselves. We can't depend on someone else to do it for us.

I believe God has a special love for each individual. Likewise, our greatest tool in reaching the lost for Christ is love. No matter who you are or what your strengths are, you can love people. Expressing that love is the best way to reach people. Love breaks down a lot of walls. You can't preach all the time. Sometimes people need something more. It doesn't take a lot to do it, but sometimes it takes a little more love.

God has given each of us a measure of love. It's our responsibility to use it. So many of us never do.

While we lived in Blue Creek, John got a job driving a bus for the local school. This gave him an opportunity to get to know the children in the area. Driving the bus came with some difficulties. Sometimes when it rained hard, the roads washed out. Even the bridges were not safe.

There was a general store on John's route called Hodges. Whenever the children had a penny they wanted to stop on the way home to buy candy. John was always patient and did whatever he could to make them happy. He certainly loved them all. I think they felt this too.

We were poor, but those were happy days.

Mary was a very serious child. One time a couple in our church was getting married. They were on their way to our house so John could marry them. Mary heard her dad and me talking about the ceremony.

She asked, "If Daddy marries Betty, who are you going to marry?"

The one thing we always had plenty of was love.

John didn't let a day go by without letting me know he loved me. Sometimes we didn't agree on everything, but we were able to understand each other and never tried to change the other's mind. We never argued. Arguing only adds fuel to the fire. On the rare occasions we had words, we quickly admitted our role in the disagreement and moved on before our anger had time to fester. We wanted a clean slate every night when we went to bed.

Pride is the biggest obstacle that can come between a husband and wife. We didn't want it to come between us or cause damage to our family.

First parsonage located in Blue Creek, Ohio.

***

Times were hard, and money was always tight. John never took an offering for himself. When a congregation took up a love offering, he was hesitant to take it. If he did, he generally put it back into the church. We never complained or brought our needs before the church. Our congregation was having it as hard as we were. Every time I had nearly reached the end of my rope and didn't see a way through the situation, God always stepped in and made a way when there was no way.

One time Calvin and Armetha came to visit with their little girl Vickie. They started blowing their horn long before they got to our house to let us know they were coming. How happy we were to see them. They climbed out of the car with their arms laden down with groceries.

Tears sprang to my eyes. We hadn't told anyone we were struggling, but I guess God did. I rejoiced in my heart. Little did I know, Calvin and Armetha had been praying for God to supply our every need. They believed God instructed them to bring those groceries to us.

Our love for each other grew stronger after that. We lived by faith during those years and learned so much.

We had killed one of the twelve chickens John's mother gave us when we left Carmel. There was a little building in the backyard we used as a chicken coop. We didn't know it at the time, but there were broken fruit jars in the building. One day Lois came running into the house and told us the chickens were eating the slivers of glass.

John and I didn't know what to do. He jumped up and went outside with Lois to see. Sure enough, they were eating the glass. We had never kept chickens before, and we didn't realize their gizzards took care of the glass or rocks or other debris they might eat. Those chickens gave us a lot of good meals.

***

At Christmastime that year, we wondered how we could afford to buy gifts for our girls. In those days department stores sent out Christmas catalogs, most notably Sears, whose catalog was called a Wish Book. Like most country kids in those days, the girls looked forward to the arrival of the Wish Book and the other store catalogs. They would lie on the floor and look through the catalogs and point out to me what they wanted.

My heart ached because I knew we didn't have any money to buy them any of the things they saw in the catalogs. I hated to think of the disappointment on their little faces on Christmas morning. I cried a little but not for long. I felt the Lord instructing me to tell the girls to choose one thing they wanted more than anything else and leave it in his hands. So I got up and did just that.

A few days later, while we were driving along the highway, we spied a little cedar tree that would make a good Christmas tree. We stopped the car, and John got out and cut it down for us.

Mary loved all kinds of animals. She even loved bugs. While John and the girls were putting up the Christmas tree in the living room, she spotted a huge bumblebee in the window. She squealed with delight and closed her hand over it. Then she let out a scream. The bug had stung her. As I soothed her tears, I knew this would work for her good. It did. That experience broke her from picking up bugs.

The day ended well though. I helped the girls make chains for the tree out of colored paper. We got the tree trimmed. In our eyes, it was the most beautiful tree on our road. The girls were so happy.

When I was a girl I wanted a dollhouse the same as my girls did, but my parents didn't have enough money to buy me one. Mom was very creative like all the Steffys. She helped me make a two-story dollhouse out of a milk crate.

I decided to do the same thing for our girls. I went to the grocery store and got an orange crate to build their dollhouse.

I put wallpaper on the inside of the crate. The girls picked out curtains from the catalogs. I also showed them how to pick out their family—a mom, dad and as many children as they wanted. We used matchboxes and Jello containers to make furniture for the house. The girls worked really hard on their project. Only one more thing was needed for their family. The girls had a wonderful time picking out clothes and outfits for the people they made. This was such a happy time for us.

I was carrying a baby at the time. Money was so tight we were at risk of having our car repossessed. John's cousin lived in another state. He felt inclined to send us a certain amount of money even though we hadn't told him anything about our financial difficulties. He sent the exact amount we needed to keep us from losing our car.

John's brother-in-law Frank Miller was led to send us twenty dollars. We took the money to town and bought each of the girls a gift for Christmas. Leona loved to carry a purse. We decided to get her one as well as things for the other girls.

The Christmas program held at the church still stands out in my memory all these years later. These precious memories will always stay in my heart. As the pastor's wife, I had to take responsibility for a lot of things I hadn't done before. It was quite a learning experience for me.

The children at the church loved to sing. Sister Lula Evans played the piano. She could only chord, but her face shone with joy as she sat at the piano. The children's voices rang out as they sang those carols and said their little parts. It was so precious. John performed the wedding ceremonies for a lot of those children after they grew up. We will always cherish those memories and the wonderful people of Blue Creek, Ohio.

On Christmas day Calvin and Armetha came through for our family again. They came driving up our road blowing the horn the way they always did. We knew who it was before they came into view. The girls ran to the window to watch.

This time when Calvin and Armetha climbed out of the car, they brought with them oranges and a lot of good things to eat. But the best thing by far—at least as far as Lois, Leona, and Mary were concerned—was a dollhouse! When the girls saw the dollhouse they squealed with delight. They couldn't wait to see what was in that store-bought dollhouse. It wasn't long before they started putting it together. The looks on their little faces made me forget all the struggles we'd been through.

I'll never forget that Christmas and all the joy it brought to our family.

John preaching from the pulpit at the church in Blue Creek.

***

Mary began having extreme difficulty cutting her teeth. She passed out at times when the tooth would break through the gum. I wasn't getting any rest, and I still had about two months to go before our baby was due. Dottie and my sister-in-law Armetha had been staying with me to help. My mother was unable to be there because she was also pregnant with my baby brother Tim.

Mary's aunt Mary and uncle Frank Miller suggested they take little Mary home with them to take care of her until after I had the baby.

The night before Easter, I heard Dottie praying in her bedroom. She ran out to the living room still shouting. The presence of the Lord engulfed me. God had told me, "You will have a son that I will use."

Soon my labor started, but there were some problems. John was getting desperate. He begged me to let him get another midwife or doctor. I told him no. I knew God was going to take care of the situation no matter how it looked to our natural eyes. The Holy Ghost came down on me. I kept saying, "Holy, Holy, Holy!" over and over again.

It wasn't long after when our baby boy was born.

My Encounters with Angels

The sun had just begun to break over the hill. It shone through the window and filled our home with our Lord's precious glory. It was Easter Sunday, April 13, 1952. They laid my little one in my arms. He was the most beautiful baby in the world. We named him Thomas Clark; Thomas after John, whose middle name was Thomas, and Clark after his uncle Calvin Clark.

When Armetha took him to bathe and dress him, she laughed and said to John, "He looks like a little old man."

John took Lois and Leona to Sunday school that morning but told them not to say anything about their new baby brother. He knew I wasn't up for company yet, and he didn't want the people of the church to stop by all day long. The girls didn't tell anyone, but they were smiling from ear to ear. I'm sure everyone at church figured it out without too much trouble.

Needless to say Tommy was the center of attention in our home. Oh, how we loved him! John was so happy to finally have a son. The girls had always teased Mary about being the baby. Now she was able to be a big sister. She was so proud.

Tommy got lots of kisses and cuddling. Mom was one of our first visitors. What a reunion it was for both of us to see each other's sons. Yes, there was lots of happiness.

***

Part of the time in Blue Creek we lived in a house owned by Sister Lula Evans' mother. Lula was such a blessing to us and the church. She was a very talented member of our congregation. She played the piano, sang songs, worked with the children, and was willing to do just about anything that needed done without complaint. We loved her, and she was highly respected by everyone who knew her.

Lula didn't live far from us. She told John and me she thought something was getting into her trash. One night Lula and her family had all gone to bed. Just as Lula was drifting off to sleep, she heard the sound of some critter in her trash.

Lula threw back the covers. She'd had enough of whatever it was making messes that she had to clean up the next morning.

Tonight would be the night she would get rid of that old dog or whatever it was.

Lula hopped out of bed and stole to the kitchen. She grabbed the broom and slipped outside. She didn't want that dog to hear her coming and run away before she could scare the ornery out of it. Even with the moon shining bright, it was dark back in those hills and Lula couldn't see a whole lot. But she saw movement so she crept closer. She reared back with her broom, and whacked that critter on the bottom with all the strength she could muster.

The critter whirled around, stood up on its back legs and came roaring at her. Lula couldn't believe her eyes. The critter she mistook for a dog foraging through her trash was a bear! It didn't take long for her to get back into the house and slam the door in the bear's face.

All the commotion woke up everyone in Lula's house. They all ran into the kitchen to find out what the racket was about. Lula was breathless and trembling and as white as a sheet. It took her a few moments to calm down enough to tell them about her adventure outside with the bear she mistook for a dog.

It didn't take long for the tale of Lula and the bear to become known all around the community. Everyone got a big laugh out of it, but they were also amazed at how brave Lula was to face that bear. Lula was a very small woman. Not the kind you would think would go up against a bear.

I still wonder if that honey bear ever came back after Lula whacked him with that broom or did he avoid her house from then on? Who knows? Maybe Lula broke him from getting into trashcans for good.

CHAPTER TEN

That summer we moved from Blue Creek to Pike County. Following my brother Tommy's death, Mom and Dad couldn't bear to keep living at their house in Elmville. It had too many painful memories for them and the boys. Dad found a property in Pike County near Beaver. He and Mom gave us a little plot of land on the property. There was a two-room building already there. We moved into that little building and John went right to work on a house for us. It was nice to be near my family again. I missed them so much, and I still worried about Mom.

At this time John was working part time as a truck driver at the atomic plant near Piketon. He also worked sometimes as a carpenter and had to be gone from home during the week. Every spare moment he had, he worked on the house he was building for our family.

With three little girls, a baby and a new house to take care of, my days were very full. Those were happy times. At church, anytime I was standing and praying or up front for something, Tommy would reach for our pastor Curtis Roberson, kneeling at the altar. I loved to tease Tommy and ask him who did something. He would say, "Dad did did did. Dad did."

Tommy dearly loved oranges and chocolate drops. John built Tommy a playpen. He would walk laps around it while I did my housework. All around the inside of the playpen were smears of sticky, chocolaty handprints where he played.

The months flew by. When Tommy was nearly nine months old he became very sick. He was always such a happy baby so I knew something was wrong anytime he fussed and cried. This was the worst I'd ever seen him. He wouldn't let me hold him against me. The doctor told me later it probably hurt Tommy and hampered his breathing when I tried to hold him against me. I was at a loss. Nothing I did could soothe him.

I had just found out my brother, Herbert, had been drinking. This broke my heart. He and I had always been so close. He loved our Tommy dearly. Every day he would stop at our house on his way home from work to play with Tommy and the girls. He always said Tommy was going to grow up to be just like him. He didn't know I had been fasting and praying for God to save him.

Two days after Tommy became so sick, I went down to Dad's garage to pray. I was so worried. My heart was also aching for Herbert. While I was praying, the Lord spoke to me as plain as day. He said, "I must take Tommy to bring Herbert in."

I stopped praying. Surely I had misunderstood. However, in my heart I knew I hadn't. I went back to the house and into the room where Tommy slept. There's nothing sweeter than a sleeping baby. He looked so precious laying there. My tears dropped onto his little face as I stood over his bed and breathed in the scent of him.

I thought of the story of Abraham and Isaac and how God changed his mind about taking Isaac once he saw Abraham's obedience. I wanted so badly for him to change his mind about taking my son. I thought if I could just get willing to lose Tommy, God might change his mind and spare my baby.

Anguish overcame me. I couldn't bear the thought of losing Tommy.

I didn't share this word from the Lord with anyone. As I suffered in my grief, Tommy's condition grew worse and worse. He had double pneumonia and pleurisy in both lungs. I had never seen such a sick baby. I continued to pray, but the situation didn't change. I knew God hadn't changed his mind.

I didn't know it at the time, but God had also shown John's mother he was going to take Tommy. She had a vision of Tommy with little wings preparing for flight.

Pastor Roberson came to the house to tell John and me we had to reach the point where we could say, "Lord, your will be done."

Knowing we needed to get to that point, and saying the words out loud, were two different things. It was one of the most difficult things we've ever had to do.

The next morning Tommy was even worse. We knew he wasn't going to make it much longer. John and I laid our precious son on our bed and sat down on either side of him. Tommy reached out and grabbed my hand. It was like he was saying, "You've been a good mommy to me."

I thought of him as a little angel who had been lent to us for a short time.

John was able to say, "Thy will be done," before I was. I took Tommy in my arms and held him and rocked him back and forth. I didn't want to let go of him. I wanted to savor the weight of him and smell of him as long as I could.

Finally the Lord gave me the strength through my grief to say, "Your will be done."

It wasn't long after that when Tommy began to labor for every breath. My brother Herbert went into town to get a doctor. The doctor said he couldn't come right then and we should bring Tommy into the office in the morning. Herbert told him Tommy might not last till morning. The doctor would not relent and did not come. John and I knew it wouldn't have made any difference if he had. God had a purpose for what he was doing with Tommy.

Again the Holy Ghost spoke through me and said, "Holy, holy, holy," as Tommy took his last breath.

Those were the same words the Spirit had spoken through me the day he was born. God was good to me, even in my pain and sorrow. I never could've made it through without his presence in my life.

Herbert came home from town that day with a heavy heart. He thought he had failed us and failed Tommy. On his way home he cried out to the Lord and gave his heart to God.

God knows what he's doing and will only do what's best. Not long after Tommy's death, God called Herbert to carry the gospel, and he preached to many through the following years. Herbert and I became closer than ever after that.

Likewise, I say unto you, there is joy in the presence of the angels of God over one sinner that repenteth.
-Luke 15:10

Tommy age 8 months

… My Encounters with Angels

CHAPTER ELEVEN

My First Encounter with an Angel

Then a woman came and told her husband saying; A man of God came unto me, and his countenance was like the countenance of an angel of God; But I asked him not whence he was, neither told he me his name. -Judges 13:6

We buried Tommy on the day he would've turned nine months old. It was a bitterly cold day. John had been laid off from work and only had one dollar in his pocket. We used that dollar to put gas in the tank to go to Sinking Springs to the funeral home. We didn't fret about it. We knew God would supply the need.

At the funeral home, a family friend I barely remembered came up to me and said, "I feel like I should give you this." It was a few folded up, wrinkled bills. John and I just stared at each other while the person walked away.

Throughout the day more people kept coming up to us and saying the same thing as they handed us money. We received enough money to pay off the funeral director and all the debt that came with burying our precious son. When we got home that night, we had ten dollars left over after we paid everything off.

God had surely supplied our every need and even more.

***

Needless to say, my grief was so great. I knew God was with me, but I didn't think I would find the strength to carry on. I had my three little girls to take care of, but my heart ached for Tommy. Nothing seemed to fill the void.

I went through the motions of caring for the girls and trying to be a good wife to John, but I missed Tommy so much. I prayed continuously for God to somehow help me with my grief.

I could barely sleep or do the chores that needed done around the house. Everywhere I looked, I saw my little Tommy. I heard his laugh and smelled his wonderful baby smell. I couldn't imagine ever suffering through a greater loss than losing my baby. My arms were so empty they physically ached to hold him one more time. I continued to seek the Lord, but I didn't think I would ever find comfort.

One night I fell into an exhausted sleep. I had a dream. It was like God let me slip into a little bit of heaven. That's when I saw my first angel.

In the dream, Tommy came walking toward me. He was holding the hand of an angel. He looked up and saw me and let go of the angel's hand. He ran to me laughing and squealing.

My heart burst with joy. I knelt on the ground, laughing and crying myself, and held out my arms. Tommy ran into my arms. He felt like life itself. I held onto him as long as I could. It was the most beautiful experience of my life. It really did take the grief away.

This dream occurred two more times. I loved it. It was so wonderful to feel my baby in my arms again.

The third time, during the dream I asked God to help me again.

The Lord said, "You must not grieve for him anymore."

Tears filled my eyes. Why didn't God understand what I was going through? "But God, he was my only son," I cried.

God sort of rebuked me. "Compare My Son to yours."

That remark helped me realize I needed to get my attention off of myself. I was so consumed with my grief and pain over

My Encounters with Angels

losing Tommy, I had taken my eyes off God and away from the family that was still here and still needed me. From then on, Heaven had a greater pull for me.

***

There was a creek on the property where we lived. The kids spent a lot of time playing there. They gathered rocks to build dams at the creek and forts and other things around the property. One day one of the kids brought a rock into the house and laid it on the floor. I stumbled over it and fell, and soon started hemorrhaging.

At first I didn't think anything of it. But the bleeding wouldn't stop. I bled off and on for ninety-one days.

As the days wore on, I grew weaker and weaker. In those days, people didn't seek medical attention for every little thing. Our answer was found in prayer. I began searching my heart to see if I had done something displeasing to the Lord. I couldn't think of anything. When my mother came to visit, I asked her to pray with me until we heard from God. The Holy Ghost spoke through her and said He was working out something more excellent in my life. I would help spread the gospel. I didn't know exactly what any of it meant, but the words comforted me greatly. I knew whatever lay ahead, God would take care of it.

I felt led to read the book of Job. God led me to Job 13:15. *Though He slay me, yet will I trust in Him, but I will maintain mine own ways before Him.*

This verse became my daily theme. I knew God was not ready to take me because my work on earth was not finished.

I continued to lose blood every day. I grew weaker and weaker and soon became bedfast. John was certainly no cook, and he wasn't much of a housekeeper. But he did the best he could. My mother and others had to take care of Leona, Lois and Mary, and cook our meals for us.

I remember one day when the hemorrhaging was especially severe. Blood gushed from my body like a fountain. It went into my armpits and into my hair before anyone could do anything to stop it. When John came home that evening, I told him I didn't think I could go through that again. No sooner had I spoke those words, I began to hemorrhage again. But this time was different. The spirit of the Lord came down on me so strong it almost lifted me off the bed. This time, instead of leaving me weak and scared, the sensation was warm and soothing. I felt like God had given me a transfusion.

I didn't get weak again. We rejoiced.

My suffering was very difficult for John. His love gave me a special anchor. We both believed we still had work to do to fulfill our purpose for the kingdom. I was sure I was dying, but there was no fear in it.

This was the first and only time in my life God gave me perfect faith. I wouldn't have made it through without him. During this time there were several people in my family, especially aunts, uncles and my brother, Herbert, who had grown cold in the Lord. God moved in their lives, and they came back to him. Even though this period was hard on John, me, and everyone close to me, the Lord was able to use me and be glorified.

The hemorrhaging wasn't my only physical problem. For some reason, every time I tried to turn over, my hips would come out of joint. This was very painful. I knew something was terribly wrong inside of me. A large knot would come up on my side. Whenever it did, it was very tender and painful to the touch.

My Second Encounter with an Angel

> *In all their affliction he was afflicted, and the angel of his presence saved them; in his love and in his pity he redeemed them; and he bore them, and carried them all the days of old.* -Isaiah 63:9

One Sunday night at the end of my second month of being bedfast, a lot of my family came to pray for me. They knew that unless God intervened I would die. Mom had been putting large layers of padding underneath me to protect the bedding from all the bleeding. That day she had to change the padding seven times.

At this point my insides were coming out of my body. It was also becoming harder and harder for me to breathe. Everyone who saw what was happening couldn't believe their eyes. I asked John to lift me up since it was so hard for me to draw a breath. I told him several times that if I seemed to die, not to get the undertaker because I would be back.

I felt my spirit leave my body. I passed out. Someone saw that I wasn't breathing anymore.

John heard that a doctor had come to visit my neighbor. He ran next door to get him. The doctor came to the house and got his stethoscope to check me. I had no blood pressure. He told John I wouldn't live till morning.

After examining me further, he told John that even if I survived, I would never have another child. I had no heartbeat for twenty minutes. Some friends of ours were praying for me at the church in Waverly. Someone in the family went there to tell them there was no need to continue praying because I was gone.

During the time I was passed out and my family thought I had died, the Lord gave me a vision.

In the vision I was standing by a river. A breeze was blowing through my hair and against my skin, rippling the surface of the water. I knew without a doubt I was standing at the River Jordan. I sensed someone behind me. I turned around to see who it was. It was an angel. I looked at him without fear. He was very large and beautiful. Maybe because I was so little, but it seemed to me like he was eight feet tall. I knew he was the angel of death, but I wasn't afraid. He reached down and took me into his arms. It was the most wonderful feeling.

We lifted off the ground and began to go higher and higher. Without him saying a word to me, I knew we were going to Heaven. We stopped at a beautiful gate. A man stood at the entrance. The brilliance inside the gate was so bright I couldn't see his countenance, but I knew it was Jesus.

He reminded me of the day Mom and I had prayed. Then he told me I would have to go back. I sure would've liked to stay there with him, but I didn't want anything to be left undone back on earth.

Jesus reached out and took hold of the angel's shoulders and turned him around to go back to the river. We slowly came back to the bed where I was laying.

I clearly remember slipping back into my body as easily as a foot slides into a shoe. The first thing I saw was John kneeling beside me praying. Thank God, he hadn't given up on me. His heart was breaking. He promised God he would do anything if the Lord would give me back to him. He said even if he only had one shirt or one pair of shoes, he would serve the Lord regardless, if the Lord would only give me back to him.

Armetha was praying on the other side of the bed. At the end of my bed, I saw my mother in a chair. Her arms were hanging limp at her sides. She was grief stricken. I don't know how long it took someone to notice my eyes were open. Once they realized it, there was a lot of rejoicing throughout the house.

I still hemorrhaged a while after that, but from then on, it felt more like a cleansing.

Afterward, I had no taste or smell for about three months. I still couldn't get up and move around. My family continued to take care of me and take care of our girls. Depression was a daily struggle. One day as I lay on the bed talking to the Lord, he spoke to me and said, "You will walk again."

That made me feel so much better. I asked him to tell me when. I didn't hear anything else from him that day. I began to wonder if I had imagined it.

A day or two later when everyone was out of the house, the Lord spoke again. "Today you will walk."

I didn't even consider my hips coming out of joint. I knew if God said it, I could do it.

Without doubting what I had heard, I swung around on the bed and put my legs over the side. It was the most movement I had done unassisted in months. I sat up and gathered my strength.

The next thing I knew I was standing at the chest of drawers, which was about four steps away from my bed. God had let me walk there all by myself. It was a wonderful moment.

My faith really began to build after that.

The next day my mom and sister-in-law were in the kitchen making dinner. Mom came into the bedroom to check on me. I said, "Mom, I'd like to walk to the couch."

She was amazed to hear it. "Oh, honey, are you sure?"

"Yes. I don't want anyone to touch me or steady me. I need to do this myself."

I was a little wobbly, but I made it with the help of the Lord.

As they finished preparing dinner, I told Mom it had been so long since I'd sat at the table. I would love to sit there and eat instead of in my room. With a little help, I made it to the table.

Just as we started to eat, I felt pressure in my stomach. Mom helped me back to the bedroom so I could use the toilet. Just as I sat down, something fell from my body. It was a stringy, horrible looking thing. The smell was so retched it took my breath away. It smelled like rotting flesh, which I guess is exactly what it was. My rotting flesh.

It was like it had been cut loose from my body. I knew the mass was what had caused my hemorrhaging. Mom gathered it up. It was about the size of both my hands held together. She threw it in the outside toilet to keep it from stinking up the house.

My healing had begun.

***

During the season of my sickness and recovery, the Lord gave my mother this assurance through the following prophesy.

> *"Are not my eyes on my daughter? My handmaiden, they are on her.*
> *Yea, tell her to fear not for I am with her. Yea, I will lift her up in my time.*
>
> *My everlasting arms are underneath her. My word shall not be broken.*

I'll not forsake or leave her alone. Yea, though fear at times do press her, tell her not to yield for I am with her. Her soul is in my hands.

Yea, and when the soul is in my hands, the body matters little. Yet I am with her in the body. Yea, she must strive to overcome the powers of afflictions.

Her life is in my hand. I am the keeper and I will deliver.

It is in the power of my hand to deliver from this world of afflictions. It is hidden with me and I shall relieve in my time.

Tell her to look up for I am. It is I that have carried her through this affliction. It is I that have carried her through. My word shall not fail."

***

While I was healing and regaining my strength, John and I prayed about what God wanted us to do. He sent us again to pastor the church in Blue Creek where we'd been when Tommy was born.

I still couldn't smell or taste so I wasn't eating right. I assumed my poor diet was the reason behind my bowel problems. I didn't see a doctor to find out for sure. We just trusted the Lord for everything.

I had always loved cornbread and buttermilk. Our food supply was getting low. There were many days I didn't know if we'd have enough food to make dinner. One day I picked up the flour sack, and there was just enough in it to make one more pone of cornbread. I prayed over it. I knew God could do anything but fail. Each day I would hold in my hands the last of the cornmeal and flour, and it was always just enough for one more batch.

The next day I would do the same thing all over again. That cornmeal lasted for three days. Each day God supplied just enough for one more batch of cornbread.

When I pulled that third day's cornbread out of the oven, it was perfectly brown and baked just right. I wished I had some fresh buttermilk to go with it. I had barely got that thought out of my head when I saw a car pull into our driveway. It was Lillian Fite, a dear friend the Lord had given me at the church.

Lillian climbed out of the car and came up through the yard, carrying something in her hands. At the door she gave me a big smile. "Sister Marjorie, Mom made some fresh butter this morning and she wanted me to bring you this quart of buttermilk."

I couldn't believe it. God had known this morning even before I did that I would want buttermilk to go with the cornbread. Once again, he had heard and answered my prayers. I was amazed and thankful he was so thoughtful of me, even in such small matters like wanting buttermilk with my cornbread. That morning my praise came from the bottom of my heart.

No cornbread and buttermilk ever tasted better. I was blessed in so many ways. Not only had the Lord used Lillian and her mother to bless me, my taste and appetite were returning.

***

John had again gotten a job driving a school bus in Blue Creek. Mary had been a Daddy's girl from the moment she was born. She loved to ride around the bus route with him as he picked up the kids for school, and would sit on the heater while he drove. To this day, she remembers going through creeks and ditches on those country roads to pick up the kids waiting for the bus.

John also worked at a stone quarry while in Blue Creek. Every chance Mary got, she would hide behind the seat of the truck in the hope of going to work with him. But I would notice her missing and go outside and get her out of the truck before John had to leave for work.

I had one more hurdle to go. My bowels still weren't moving regularly. I vomited nearly everything I ate. I hated to complain, and I didn't want John to know how bad I felt.

Finally I broke down and told him I didn't think I could take it anymore. Even though I was so sick, I didn't want to go to the doctor.

We both prayed until we prayed through to victory. God told us, "I will heal what the cancer has eaten." And He did!

CHAPTER TWELVE

Sister Hattie Roberson, a widow from Cooksville, Tennessee, began asking God to send a Pentecostal minister to bring Pentecost to her area of Tennessee. She asked John and me to join her in prayer over this matter. We prayed with her several times about it. She was a wonderful, committed sister in the Lord, and we loved her very much. While we were praying with her and seeking the Lord, we had no idea God would use us to fulfill Sister Hattie's petition.

One day God gave us a choice. He said we could go to Tennessee and suffer for the kingdom, or John could keep his job and prosper beyond measure. But we would miss the Rapture.

It was a big decision we didn't take lightly, but it didn't take long for us to decide to pack up and head to Tennessee. God told us we had till the twentieth day of August to get there.

Someone had given John a pig, and it became our pet. We couldn't think of eating that pig like we first planned. Instead we decided to sell it and get all three girls winter coats for our trip.

On the way to Tennessee we stopped in Kentucky at a spring to let the girls stretch their legs and get a drink. The girls were so proud of their new coats they wanted to wear them even though the day wasn't very cold. Lois stepped on a slick rock and fell in the edge of the spring. She was so upset about getting her new coat wet, she just sat there in the water.

We finally got to Sister Hattie's and forgot about the wet coat ordeal. The few weeks we were there we lived with Sister

Hattie.

She had a four-year-old grandson named Jerry. One day I was lying on the couch while Jerry and Mary were playing and running around it. The two of them were quite a contrast. Jerry had dark hair with big brown eyes. Mary had curly blonde hair with blue eyes.

Jerry said, "Mary, I want you be my girlfriend, not my sweetheart."

Mary wasn't interested. "No," she said.

Jerry wasn't ready to give up that easily. "Well, if you will be my sweetheart, you have to come and live with me."

She thought about it a moment and then relented. "Okay," she said.

I couldn't help but laugh. When I wrote to Mom that week, I asked if she thought three-years-old was a bit young to get your first proposal. I didn't let Mary go stay with Jerry's family, but they continued to be good friends as long as we lived there.

***

While in Cooksville our family lived on sixty dollars a month. Our dedication was really tested during that time.

We faced many tough times while living in Tennessee, but God always proved faithful.

One lady in the church believed that because we were from Ohio, we thought we were superior to her and the congregation. That broke my heart. I did what I could to minister to her and be a friend, but none of my efforts seemed to touch her.

I didn't have many clothes to wear. I had an old skirt I had patched to wear to church. Try as I might, I couldn't get that patch to blend in with the rest of the fabric so it wasn't so obvious. I didn't have any choice but to wear it anyway. When I sat down near the woman who thought I was proud, that old patch showed up as plain as day. The woman looked down at the patch. Then she looked at me. I could see in her eyes that God used the patch to show her we were just humble people the same as everyone else in the church.

She and I were friends from then on.

My Encounters with Angels

God sent us to minister to many humble homes of people who lived on the mountain in Cooksville. We soon found out what he meant by suffering. We told no one of our suffering, but God knew we were willing to suffer. Many times while we lived there we would get down to a bag of potatoes and nothing else to eat. I learned how to cook potatoes in every way imaginable. God was faithful, and we never went hungry. But, boy, did I get tired of cooking potatoes.

There was a neighbor who lived on the other side of Sister Hattie's. She had a turnip patch. She told me I could help myself to as many turnips and turnip greens as I wanted. Those turnips sure tasted good with the potatoes.

Mary got sick while we were there, but we knew God would take care of her. Sister Hattie had a cellar house, and Mary loved going into the cellar with her. Each time she came back, she had a can of Sister Hattie's peaches in her arms. No peaches ever tasted as good as those did.

Our car broke down. Sister Hattie felt to give us some money, but still no one knew our problems. It was just between God and us. The money was just enough to do the work to get the car running. Then one day when I was cleaning my kitchen, I saw an oat cereal box. I started to throw it away, but as I shook it, it felt like there was something in it. I opened it and found a ten-dollar bill. I took it and went to the nearby grocery store and got the necessary things. We came home happy.

The Lord performed many miracles while we were there. One time a woman sent for us. Her little girl had died. We had never seen the woman before and didn't know who she was. But she had heard we were praying people.

When we got there she was sitting in a chair clinging to the baby and crying. She would not lay the baby down. She just kept rocking back and forth and saying, "The Lord's going to give me my baby back."

We prayed with her for the longest time. She kept crying and repeating her words while John and I continued to pray. Suddenly we saw life in that little girl. Another of the woman's children had come into the room and was sitting on the floor with an apple. When the little one woke up, she wanted the apple. We were all so shocked. We worried about giving her the apple because she had been unconscious for so long.

John said, "Whatever God wants her to have we must give her."

***

Calvin and Armetha were always such a blessing to us. They had brought their small mobile home to Tennessee for us to live in. We felt such love from them. They sacrificed their trailer for us and moved in with John's parents to take care of them.

The months passed and it came time for another Christmas. Sister Hattie had sold her place, and we felt clear to come home for Christmas. We piled the kids and our clothes into the car and headed for Ohio. After we got home, I became sick. My mother, John's parents, and his brother were praying for me. God spoke through my mother and said because we were faithful through our suffering, we would never suffer like that again. God let us suffer things as others did so we would not be too quick to judge.

Later John and one of my brothers went to bring Calvin and Armetha's trailer back from Tennessee. When they got to the most treacherous part of the mountain, the brakes went out on John's car that was pulling the trailer. They kept going toward home praying every mile. God brought them home safe and sound. How great our God is!

1954

Curtis and Rosie Roberson were pastors at the Carmel Church of God. At the time, we lived in Beaver in the house John built for us that Mary called the white house. It was Christmas Day, and I felt an urgency to go to Rosie. I couldn't shake it. I told John I felt like I needed to go see her no matter what.

He gave me one of those looks like husbands do. "Honey, its Christmas. Just wait till tomorrow."

I tried to shake the urgency that kept working on me, but it wouldn't ease off. I told myself John was right and nobody wanted unexpected company on Christmas Day.

A little while later Calvin showed up at our door. He had come from the Roberson's house.

"Rosie's labor has started," he told us. He looked at me. "She's calling for you. She wants you with her."

That explained the urgency I felt. Without a moment's hesitation, I jumped into Calvin's car and we headed to the Roberson's. As I opened the back door to go inside, the presence of the Lord fell upon me. The closer I got to Rosie's room, the stronger and stronger the Lord's covering grew. It was as though I was completely covered by the Spirit of the Lord.

In the bedroom, Dottie was tending Rosie. It was apparent both women were worn out and stressed. The baby wasn't coming. Dottie had ascertained the cord was wrapped around the baby's neck. A delivery now would be deadly if she couldn't untangle the cord.

Dottie and Rosie had been working for hours and had nearly reached their limit. Dottie's hands were shaking so badly from fatigue, she couldn't get the cord unwound from the baby's neck. When she looked up and saw me, she nearly collapsed in relief. She was practically in tears.

She stepped back so I could take over. She wiped a tired arm across her brow as she told me what to do. I prayed for wisdom and strength and then went to work following Dottie's instructions.

We still had a long way to go, but finally little Curtis Roberson Junior made his way into the world. It was a beautiful moment. Rosie cried and laughed at the same time as she snuggled her little son against her. Dottie was so thankful the whole thing was over and we had a safe delivery.

I took little Curtis from his proud mama and gave him his first bath. I couldn't stop smiling at this little one in my lap. I was so thankful God had directed me there that day so I could be part of helping him into the world.

As I bathed him, he kept turning his head as if to ask, "Where am I? How did I get here?" I think it was then I gave him his first kiss. From that moment on, I felt a bond with him that lasts till this day. Curtis was just so special.

He's a grown man now with a family of his own. He's possibly even a grandpa. John and I dearly loved the Roberson family. They have always been a very special family to us and have meant so much to us over the years. Before little Curtis Jr. came along, the Robersons had a daughter, Colitcha. She became a nurse when she grew up. Their next child was David. Years later when he heard I had fallen down the stairs and had to have a hip replacement, he and his wife Jan came to see us.

David said he wasn't going to leave our house until he put a handrail along the stairway to the second floor and another one along the stairs to our basement. What a wonderful blessing his thoughtfulness was to me.

I ask the Lord to bless David and his family every time I go up and down those stairs. We had prayer before they left that day, and I could feel their parents' ministry going on through David and Jan's hands as they have touched John's and my life.

Patricia was the Roberson's next child. She was their singer, songwriter, and a minister to many. Rose and Curtis have gone on to be with the Lord, but what a heritage they left for their children. I pray for the family daily.

CHAPTER THIRTEEN

One beautiful day the following summer, we took our kids to the Cincinnati Zoo. This was the first time they had been to the zoo. Mary was about three-years-old and loved monkeys. We headed to the exhibit to watch the chimpanzees do their tricks. John set Mary on his shoulders so she could see over everyone's heads. Lois, Leona, and I found a place in the crowd on the opposite side of John and Mary to watch. The chimps were riding bikes and doing tricks. It was so cute.

Then I noticed John didn't have Mary on his shoulders anymore. I took the girls over to see where she was. When I got to John, I asked him where Mary was.

He looked around the large crowd. "Well, I don't know. She saw you and wanted to go to you."

My heart dropped. We didn't know what to do. I called out to the Lord to help us find her. To my dismay, I spotted our Mary sitting on the ground between two chimpanzees. One chimp was pulling out her curls and watching them spring back against her head. Mary didn't seem to mind. She was holding the other chimp's hand in hers and checking it out.

John and I hurried over to the wall and got the zookeeper's attention. He picked Mary up and brought her to us. She was reluctant to leave the chimpanzees.

I told John to not let go of her hand for the rest of the day. I think Mary left a little piece of her heart with those chimps that day. For a long time afterward, she saved her money with the intention of buying her own. Thank the Lord she never reached her goal. I had my hands full enough taking care of three little girls who sometimes acted like monkeys. I had no energy for the real thing.

***

While my little family was growing up, so were my brothers as they began having families of their own. My third brother, Elisha, married a girl named Ruth from Oregonia. John performed the ceremony under a canopy of shade trees at Fort Hill State Park near Sinking Springs. It was a beautiful day for a wedding. The entire family was there. We enjoyed spending the day together, laughing, eating, and wishing the newlyweds well.

Elisha Elden Powell with his new bride Ruth.

***

The following winter, my cousin Wilmer Steffy had just gotten out of the Air Force and bought a car. He wanted to show it off to Herbert, so he came to take him for a drive. Herbert had been struggling with his sight for years following the gunshot accident. He had lost eighty percent of his eyesight in the accident. At this time when Wilmer got out of the service, the government was building the atomic plant in Pike County. It was January 1954, and the roads were slick with ice. Wilmer and Herbert were driving along Germany Road in the direction of the Atomic Plant. Wilmer picked up speed to gain traction to go over a hump in the road. One of the work trucks from the atomic plant was coming the other way. Neither vehicle had anywhere else to go to get out of each other's way. They hit head on.

The collision threw Herbert into the rearview mirror and tore the retinas loose from his eyes. A school bus was following the car, and the kids on the bus saw the accident. They saw Herbert's face, and probably still remember the image.

The doctors wanted to try one last surgery to save Herbert's sight. He stayed in the hospital for three weeks. While he was at the hospital his left eye kept swelling because of blood clots behind it. They tried to operate on it, but it was no use. They ended up having to remove both eyes.

Herbert and his wife Ruth lived with Mom and Dad for a while after the accident. One morning Mom went into the bedroom, and Herbert couldn't move. Tears were running down his face, but he couldn't move. She remembered what the doctor said after he had been shot. The buckshot might come loose and work its way into his brain. If that happened, he would be paralyzed. She feared what the doctors said may have happened She started praying for him, and Herbert received a miracle and was able to walk and talk again.

Losing his sight did not slow Herbert down. He attended a blind school in Columbus where he was at the top of his class so they made him an instructor. He worked for the government at the farm school and operated a dairy in Mason. Work kept him away from the family for up to a month at a time so he quit to find a position closer to home.

Eventually he became a preacher. He ministered at the Church of God in Blue Creek. He helped remodel the Lucasville Church of God and held the first revival there.

Herbert Reeves Powell with his seeing eye dog.

Herbert loved to tell us of adventures he had while at the blind school in Columbus. He was always a strong willed person. When he tackled something, he gave it his all. Learning how to do everyday things at the blind school was no different.

One of the many things he did there was training with a seeing eye dog he named Toby. Herbert and Toby had to learn to work together and sometimes it didn't always go the way it was meant to go. Toby would run Herbert into poles. Herbert got tired of that trick so he ran Toby into a pole. That ended the two of them running into poles.

During training sessions they would go on practice runs together. One day while they were out training, Toby led Herbert across a set of railroad tracks. Herbert knew the route they were meant to take didn't have any railroad tracks. They were lost. But with his good instincts, Toby at his side, and the Lord's help, they made it back to the blind school.

Herbert operated a concession stand in front of the post office to earn money. People were always coming and going in and out of the building and Herbert was always busy selling them food. One day some men approached Herbert. Toby jumped to his feet. The hair on the back of his neck stood up, and he growled deep in his throat. Herbert was sure the men were intent on robbing him. Otherwise he knew Toby wouldn't have reacted that way. He reached down and let Toby loose. Off the dog went after them. All Herbert could hear was the sound of fast moving feet running away from his concession stand. It wasn't long before Toby came back. They never had any trouble after that. Toby was a good and faithful friend.

Herbert had several seeing eye dogs over the years. Another one I remember very well was named Hilda. She was a lovely white German Shepard dog. Hilda didn't like the sound of a chain, and she couldn't be trained. Herbert asked if we would take her. We were living in the country at the time where Hilda had plenty of space to run free the way she wanted.

She was very loving to our family. When I did our wash and hung the clothes out on the line, Hilda always kept the other dogs and cats away from me.

Herbert and his wife Ruth had three children. Roger is the oldest. John gave Roger his first haircut while he was sitting in his high chair. He is in the ministry and works at a stone quarry. I always loved to collect interesting rocks. One time when he came to visit, he gave me a special rock.

I'll never forget one pretty July day when John and I went to visit Herbert and Ruth. While we were there, Ruth went into labor and had to go to the hospital. Before they left I told her she would have a little red-headed firecracker. Within hours she gave birth to their daughter Peggy Lee. She is now Herbert's health caregiver. She writes beautiful poems and letters to witness and encourage prisoners, family, and friends.

Herbert's son, Larry, works in the printing industry. He is very skilled in his profession. I remember one Christmas that he designed and made all of us beautiful Christmas cards. I treasured mine for years.

***

I never forgot the doctor's words while I was suffering with my cancer that if I survived, I would never have another baby. Our arms had been so empty since Tommy's death. But I didn't dwell on the doctor's prognosis or on my emptiness without Tommy. The Lord was always my strength and my comfort. I had a loving husband, three beautiful little girls, and a strong church family. I was blessed beyond measure. I didn't know the Lord was about to bless me even more.

When Mary was five-years-old, I realized I was going to have another baby. John and I were so excited. We knew this baby would be our miracle baby.

I was happy the whole time I was pregnant. I could hardly wait to find out what I was carrying. Of course John wanted a boy, but I felt another girl would fit in just fine. John didn't want me to try to have this baby without a doctor so we went to stay with John's parents until the baby was born.

Finally the day we waited for arrived. It was November 24th, 1956. John called Dr. Cutwright from Bainbridge, who came to the house for the delivery the way doctors did in those days.

The pain was so great, I passed out during the delivery. The doctor said, "We must get this baby here." He helped push the baby from my body.

How happy I was to have my little miracle child. I looked at John and asked what it was.

Tears of joy rolled down his cheeks. "It's another little girl."

I could see he was disappointed, but it wasn't long before she would win his heart. I let John name her. He decided on Rebecca Rose. I cannot tell you how happy we were.

Rebecca sure filled the vacancy left by her brother.

Mary said, "Now I am a big sister!" She lived up to being a big sister in lots of ways.

When I had been praying for my brother Herbert to be saved all those years ago, I had a vision. In the vision I saw a baby. I didn't know at the time what it meant. As I was dressing Rebecca for church that first Sunday after her birth, I realized she was the baby I had seen in my vision. She was even wearing the same clothes. I couldn't believe it. God was so good. My heart was full, and I finally had another little baby to fill my empty arms.

***

Carmel Church of God

The congregation Dottie Reed started over the Rhodes Grocery Store in Sinking Spring soon outgrew that little room and needed to spread its wings. They proceeded to build the Carmel Church of God, which was the first Pentecostal church in the area. Otis Rich, a circuit rider from Wilmington who traveled the area on horseback and preached wherever he could, contributed the very first dollar to build the church. Back then, a dollar was a lot of money to donate.

Dottie endured much persecution while starting the church. Members of another denomination put hateful letters in local mailboxes, warning residents against the evil influence of Pentecost. Despite their efforts to spread fear and hatred, the little church flourished. Years later, one of the individuals involved in writing the letters against Dottie and the church suffered a tragedy in his own life. Wouldn't you know it, he turned to Dottie for consolation and advice. So God was triumphant!

John and I were ministering at Blue Creek and evangelizing at the time. Despite the long distance between Carmel and Blue Creek, John felt led to help work on the basement of the Carmel church that summer so it would be ready before winter. He built the pulpit and worked hard every chance he got.

John's sister-in-law, Armetha, and I mixed batches of concrete in wheelbarrows so it would be ready when the workers were ready to pour. Stirring concrete sure was a lot different than mixing a cake at home. I was so tired and sore by the time I got home every night, but it sure was a blessing to be able to help out.

The congregation had a beautiful belfry built for the church. Frank Miller, one of John's brothers-in-law, purchased a bell from one of the local schools to go in the belfry. Frank rang that bell for many years. Its lovely notes rang out over the community as if to say, "We're here. Come worship with us." No one could take hold of that rope that hung down from the belfry and make the bell ring the way Frank could.

Dottie loved to preach the Word. When she got under the anointing it seemed like she would glide across the floor waving her handkerchief. It was a beautiful sight to see. It was hard not to get happy along with her when the Lord took hold of her. Over time she got so she would take coughing spells in church. Someone would have to take her home so she could rest. It wasn't much longer before she realized she couldn't continue preaching. When Dottie needed to step down, the Church of God overseers asked John and I if we would take over the congregation in Carmel.

We bought a house near the church and became the pastors. We held our first service on Father's Day. John and I were honored to serve the Lord and his people as pastors. John would play the mandolin and we would sing. One of our favorites songs to sing together was *It's Worth it All*.

Kenneth Miller was a very supportive member of our congregation in Carmel. One of the things he did was make sure the church had enough fuel oil to last through our long Ohio winters. Kenneth was married to John's sister, Martha. She played the piano for us for many years. After she stepped down, her daughter June Thompson took her place. June also played the piano after we moved to the Hillsboro Church of God. When Martha's son was a baby, she would have to take him to the basement when he got noisy because there was no nursery for the children.

Bill Brandenburg and his family played instruments and sang for us. Richard and Marian Walls were faithful to bring their family to church and also sang specials. My aunt Marie Powell was a steady and strong supporter of our congregation. You will read more about her later in this book.

Marie's daughter Olive played the piano. Martha taught her that. She also sang like a bird. Their son attended with them and supported the church. When the Lord blessed Aunt Marie's husband Mack, he would hop up and down as he praised the Lord. It just made you happy to watch him.

I've seen many couples married in our churches over the years, but I'll never forget Arnold and Frances McCleese's wedding. I thought Frances was one of the most beautiful brides I'd ever seen.

Arnold was a talented musician. He played his guitar and harmonica for us in church. As time went by, their family grew. They raised their children in church, all of them singing with beautiful voices to the Lord. It was always so uplifting when they came to our house to visit.

How good God is to us. There have been so many precious church family members and pastors that meant so much to us—too many to mention here. Just know I love you all.

First service at Carmel Church of God on Father's Day.

One of our faithful families in the Carmel congregation was the Scotts. They had eleven children, just like my parents. We loved to hear them sing together as a family. I'll never forget the Sunday their son Jerry came to church to show off his new car. He had just gotten out of the service and was so proud and riding high, anticipating impressing the girls with his new wheels. On the very last turn of the road as the church came in sight, he hit a skunk. Needless to say, none of the girls were interested in going for a ride in his new car that day.

***

Our daughter Rebecca began singing in church when she was three. One night, when she was older, John said if anyone needed anything from the Lord, they should come and stand at the altar. Rebecca went straight to the front. She told her daddy she wanted him to anoint her hands with oil so God would help her be able to play the piano.

Everywhere she went after that, if there was a piano or an organ, she would try to play it. She could pick up how to play a song after hearing it. We knew God's hand was on her.

Her grandmother's old upright piano had been given to us. As a teenager, anytime Rebecca was battling a problem, she would go upstairs to pray about it when she got home from school. After she would get victory over the situation, she would sit down at the piano and play till she started rejoicing. It was an amazing thing to see.

While we lived in Carmel, we would go to town on Saturdays to do our shopping. John gave the girls money every time he could. One time he gave Rebecca a dollar. She thought and thought what she would buy with her money. She finally decided to buy a goldfish. We had sulfur water at our house. It smelled really bad and didn't taste too good either. I made a lot of Kool-aid just so the girls would drink the water. Rebecca thought about the water and asked if the fish would survive in it.

John told her, "Honey, I don't know, but I don't think so."

Rebecca thought about his words for a moment and replied, "Well, some people know and some people think." That gave John the title for a sermon the following Sunday. *Some people know and some people think.*

***

We rented a parsonage on Roundhead Rd outside of Hillsboro, Ohio while we pastored a little church on Beech Street. We learned later that the previous residents had moved out of the house because they believed it was haunted.

Even though we didn't believe the house was haunted, we couldn't deny the strange noises at all hours of the night. We often heard scratching, squealing, and what sounded like fighting. We didn't know what to think.

John told me and the girls there was nothing to it. We shouldn't let it bother us. But the girls' imaginations were running rampant. One morning as I was getting John's breakfast before he left for work, we heard strange sounds coming from the basement. John jumped up and threw open the door that led to the basement, but there was complete silence. John said, "I'm getting out of this place." He was my hero up until that happened.

After church one night we heard a noise.

Lois said, "Daddy, look there!"

It was raccoons! They were peeking out of the register above our woodstove. We could see their little fuzzy paws enjoying the heat. The girls got the bright idea to feed them bread with jelly on it. John looked around to see how the coons got in so he could remedy the situation. The next time our landlord came to the house, I told him about the raccoons and the ruckus they made. He said he was so glad we didn't think the house was haunted and move out like everyone else had.

***

We had other visitors at that house that weren't as pleasant as the raccoons. A family of groundhogs moved in under the house. One night they got into a fight and made a terrible racket. It was spooky. I was brave as long as John was home, but I didn't feel brave after he left for work.

One time when Evelyn Brewer and Frankie McConnahey

were visiting, the groundhogs got into another fight and began screeching and screaming at each other. Our company was terrified. They left in such a hurry, one of them left behind a shoe in fresh tar next to the road.

While he was mowing the yard a few days later, John saw some boards missing off the side of the house. He tracked the groundhogs and figured out where they were going in and out and fixed the problem.

My Encounters with Angels

CHAPTER FOURTEEN

Grandma Cora Steffy

Grandpa Steffy had married his first wife Alma, and they had Monta and the older children. After Alma's death from tuberculosis, Grandpa Steffy went to see if he could find some of her family. He went to the house where Alma's adopted parents lived. In the yard, he saw Alma's younger sister Cora blacking an old cook stove. In those days that's how they prepared stoves for the winter months when they were used inside the house.

Cora had nearly as much blacking on herself and her clothes as she did the stove. Grandpa was a jolly fellow who liked to laugh, and he thought the sight of Cora was very funny. At the time, he didn't realize he would fall in love with the young woman and she would become his next wife and the mother of his children.

Like all the Steffys, Grandpa was very talented. He painted portraits on mirrors. While he was still married to Alma, he painted a life-size portrait of her. Aunt Monta was so proud of that picture. She didn't remember much about her biological mother, and the painting meant a lot to her. One time she wanted to show it to company. While she was carrying it to them, she stumbled and broke the mirror with the portrait.

Grandpa was very upset. He gave Monta a whipping because the portrait couldn't be replaced. That whipping broke Monta's heart. She never got over it. Grandpa didn't realize what his reaction did to her. All he could see was the loss of the painting. The punishment meant much more than that to Monta.

Monta missed her biological mother her entire life. Alma always held a special place in Monta's heart. But Monta grew to love Cora as much as she could ever love a biological mother.

The following article was written by Monta in honor of Cora Steffy and published in The Church of God's Evangel Magazine on May 8, 1966.

I Called Her Mother

Many fine tributes and honors are given to mothers on Mother's Day, and rightly so. But I've often wondered why so little is said of the thousands of stepmothers who so justly deserve credit for filling a mother's place in a little child's life.

My mother died when I was two-years-old. When my father remarried, he gave me the finest second mother a child ever had. When her own little ones were born (she had seven), she taught each one to call me, "Sister". To this day they call me that, and I'm "Aunt Sister" to all the nieces and nephews. She never allowed me to feel I was only a half-sister to the others.

Looking back over the past sixty years I can see so many precious things she gave me. She taught me about God and His care for us. We were very poor, but we were also wealthy because we had so much happiness at home. She made the most of what we had, and sometimes that was very little, but we were never made to feel we were deprived of the good things in life just because we were poor.

She showed us there was beauty all around us, but that it was most important to have it within. Her hands were not beautiful as some would count beauty; they were rough, toil-worn hands. But they had a special beauty all their own for us.

One year we wanted valentines for our valentine box at school. Not having money to buy them was no problem for us. Our mother *made* them. She cut pretty shapes from white cardboard, scalloped the edges (and not with pinking shears either), and wrote little verses on them. Then she took the tiny red flowers from her one and only summer hat and somehow wove them through the cardboard. We gave the prettiest valentines of all. Even the teacher wanted to know where our mother learned to do that. I was so proud of her!

Our clothes were all handmade because she had no sewing machine. When she bought material for our school dresses, she always let me choose the piece I wanted first.

She is the one who pointed out to me the beauty of the stars and the lovely colors in nature, even those in old Mr. Wooly Worm's fuzzy coat. She taught me there was beauty in storms, and through her I learned to love them. She enjoyed working with bits of clay, and I have an Indian head she molded from red clay. I have had it for fifty-five years and shall keep it until it crumbles into dust. It is lovely that her dear hands made it.

She was never too busy to stop and look at a leaf or stone or feather we would bring to her. Usually she could tell us something interesting about it.

I remember a family who moved near us. They were very poor and always seemed to be so "alone". No one paid much attention to them. When their little baby died, Mother felt so sorry for them she made a wreath of her garden flowers and ferns. I took it to their house, and it was all they had. Somehow I had the feeling that the mother understood and was comforted a little. I know our mother put all the prayers and love and sympathy possible into that wreath. It was her quiet, gentle way of showing that someone cared.

She taught us about God and read His precious Word to us. Every day we looked for a miracle, for something beautiful—and found it. Because she taught us that God *expected* us to see Him in every day of our lives. Early morning was her favorite time of day. It held so much promise. It was so new.

When she left us at Easter time, she was eighty-three years old. We laid her to rest beside our father in an early morning service. God had washed the world the night before. Everything was new and clean, and for her, an eternal day had dawned.

She is gone, but she has left me some very precious memories. One thing she believed in—God has a "David" for every "Goliath" we will ever have to face in this life. What more could a mother leave to a child?

Some called her my stepmother.
I called her mother.

by Monta Maria Houck

***

Years later I went down to take care of Mom. She had been hospitalized with a rheumatic heart and had enough gallstones to pave the driveway. Grandpa Steffy had passed away years earlier leaving Cora all alone. I don't know if she quite knew what to do with herself without Grandpa and a bunch of kids to take care of. Grandma Cora called a taxi to take her from Lebanon, Ohio to Mom's house in Pike County. We were all surprised by the cost of that taxi ride.

Grandma Cora never had much of a childhood. Her adopted family gave her a fine education, but they didn't give her the love a little girl needed. They didn't have children of their own, and they were very strict with her.

The very first evening I was at Mom's to take care of her while she recovered from her gallstones, I heard a commotion down by the corncrib. There was a big metal barrel, and Grandma Cora was beating on it like a drum. The boys had built a fire and were challenging each other to see who could get closest to it. Grandma was supposed to be an Indian and was adding drama to the evening. If something could be dangerous, she was all for it. I had to make them put out the fire before someone got hurt. The boys and Grandma could come up with all kinds of dangerous situations.

When it got dark on the farm you went to bed because you'd been working hard the whole day and were tired. One night I couldn't understand why the boys were so noisy. I went to investigate. They had turned the beds in a row so they could somersault from one bed to the next. Just as I entered the room, Grandma was poised on the first bed ready to jump. She was heavy and not very small and getting older. I was afraid she would hurt herself.

Whenever she was at Mom's around my brothers, she became a kid all over again.

Dad had a wagon the boys pulled behind a tractor to haul corn and other things. Grandma and the boys would give each other rides in it. They liked to have contests to see how fast they could make the tractor go. It was funny to see Grandma bouncing along in that wagon. The more exciting a situation was, the more likely Grandma would be in the middle of it.

She bought Johnny and Tim BB guns. They got so they would shoot each other with them. When Mom was feeling stronger, she hid the BB guns. The boys searched the house high and low, but they never found them.

I became afraid Grandma would get hurt. I couldn't decide if the boys were a bad influence on her or if she was a bad influence on them. We decided it was time for her to go live with Aunt Katherine.

I was too busy helping Mom recuperate and keeping the boys out from under her feet. I couldn't take care of all of them. It was too much for me. Grandma was so happy with the boys. I hated to hurt her that way, but there was no way to take care of all of them. She really kept the boys stirred up. There were no hard feelings, but I hated to do it.

Aunt Katherine welcomed Grandma back to her home.

It wasn't much longer after Grandma Cora went to Katherine's that she passed away. She and Katherine were in the bedroom talking. Cora was combing her hair. Then she just slumped over and died. God had taken her gently. Now she's in heaven having fun.

CHAPTER FIFTEEN

Mom's health never fully recovered after her gallstone surgery. By the following year she was very ill.

In late May, 1962 she was admitted to University Hospital in Columbus. Every morning I rode to the hospital with John's brother, Albert, who worked in Columbus. He would drop me off at the hospital on the way to work. I would sit at Mom's bedside until Albert picked me up in the evening on his way home.

Most of the time, Mom was too weak to talk. I sat next to her day after day and held her hand and talked to her.

The nurses at the hospital thought so much of my mother. May 21st, 1962 was Mom's fifty-second birthday. The nurses planned a surprise party for her.

She would've been so pleased to know how much they cared for her and how much trouble they went to preparing for her birthday party there. However, on that day she became gravely ill. She didn't know anything that was going on, and she didn't recognize any of us.

Mom's older brother, Charles, and his wife Ethel came to see her. They brought her a comb, a brush and some house slippers for a birthday gift. This was a true answer to prayer. It meant so much to her. Uncle Charles seemed to realize she could go at anytime. That day God rekindled their love for one another as brother and sister.

After Uncle Charles and Aunt Ethel left, I lovingly brushed Mom's hair the best I could. The next day Mom told me her brother, Herbert, his wife Verna and their youngest son, Jerry were coming to visit her. I thought maybe it was just wishful thinking or she really didn't know what was going on. She hadn't talked on the phone to anyone, and she couldn't know who would be coming to see her.

But Mom told me the Lord had told her they were coming.

Mom was so happy at the prospect of seeing Uncle Herbert. They had always been close to each other. It really brightened her day. Needless to say, I was shocked when they walked through the door. Mom grinned from ear to ear as she reached out to Uncle Herbert. He took her hand and kissed it and said, "Molly, I love you."

Molly was the nickname the Steffy family called Mom.

It wasn't long after that I had to stop going to see her for a while. I was so exhausted and run down, I was unable to see her for one week. I knew she would miss seeing me, and she'd worry if she knew I was feeling bad.

I prayed for God to give me the strength to see her one more time before it was eternally too late. None of us knew how much longer Mom had. I called Albert and asked him to pick me up the next morning. John was worried I was pushing myself too hard, but I didn't have a choice. I had to get back to the hospital.

I'm so glad I did. When I walked into her hospital room, I walked straight into the presence of the Lord. Mom was smiling. She looked like an angel. When she saw me, she said, "My precious daughter."

My heart swelled with love for her. I put my hand under the oxygen tent and grasped her hand. I put it to my lips and kissed it.

She said, "Oh, Marjorie, they called my name this morning!"

I knew what she meant. She would be going to heaven soon. I knew I would miss her, and my life would never be the same. But the glory of the Lord was so strong all over Mom and all over that room, I could not even grieve.

There was a Catholic lady in the room with Mom. She and Mom had gotten to know each other pretty well. The woman told me, "Oh, honey, we don't have to worry about where your mother is going."

It made me feel better to know Mom had been a witness to everyone she met while she was in the hospital.

While Mom was in the hospital, the Holy Ghost would come down on her, and she would sing in tongues. Then she would sing the same words in English. One nurse kept being late for her classes because she didn't want to leave Mom's room. God allowed Mom to read from the Book of Life and see some of the names in it. She was so happy to tell me she saw my name and John's name there.

It seemed like we were all so close to heaven during that time. It was like the presence of the death angel was there to take Mom home. She was so happy. We couldn't grieve for her. We knew she was going to glory any moment, any second. I felt like I could have shouted all over the room.

Mom became sick with a terrible case of pneumonia. Her kidneys had begun to shut down, but the pneumonia was the last thing to push her over the edge. God let John's mother, who had already passed away, come to visit Mom. They had been dearest of friends in life. It meant so much to Mom to see Dottie again before joining her in heaven.

Dottie's nickname was Mawsie. Her son Calvin started calling her that when he was a young man, and it caught on with the rest of the family. Calvin had a habit of nicknaming people. When Mom saw Dottie in her vision, she cried out, "Oh, Mawsie, you've come!" Then she thanked her for something, but I couldn't tell what it was.

After that Mom never asked for another drink of water. I wondered if the Lord had allowed Dottie to give Mom a drink of heavenly water.

Dad and the boys came up to visit Mom for a while. It was a special and happy time together as a family. Mom was able to kiss each one of us goodbye. Mom and I had a wonderful day together. She had been sick and weak for a long time, but that day she was able to talk to me all day long. It was such a blessing. It was our last day on earth together.

After Dad and the boys left, Mom looked at me. "The one I worry about most is Johnny. He will serve the Lord and go deep or he will go deep into the depths of sin."

Again she read off some of the names she had seen in the Lamb's Book of Life. She would speak to me in tongues for a while, and then she would interpret what she said.

Finally it was time for me to leave. Later that evening at home as it was getting dark, someone came from Martha's house and told us to call the hospital. A peace filled my heart. I knew the call was about Mom. I also knew what it meant. I hurried over and made the call. Someone from the hospital told us my dear mother had passed away.

I went limp inside. I didn't know what I'd do without her. I grieved my loss of her. There was an emptiness at knowing I could never talk with her again. I could never turn to her when I needed a mother's love and compassion.

That left me to take Mom's place for my brothers. I was the oldest and the one expected to step in and be a mother to them.

No matter how hard it was to lose my precious mother, I'm so glad God allowed us that last glorious day together. I'll never forget it.

***

My mother was such a wonderful woman who lived her entire life for the Lord. Everything was dedicated to him since the moment she met Jesus. When I was a kid I wanted to be just like her. The following is the last prophesy my mother prophesied over me. She was always such an amazing person and taught me so much. It means so much to me to share this prophesy with you.

Last prophecy from Mary Powell

Dated August 27, 1961

"Unto thee, Marjorie, to whom I am speaking.

Stand fast. Stand fast. Thou art a vessel to leave weak that you might be strong. Yet I will use thee many days, and there shall be signs to go forth from the power that lives within thee. Compromise not. That, that is within is strong, not only in works, but in teaching and healing and miracles. You shall be strength to thy husband. I am pleased with you. Rejoice. Your soul and spirit are in my hands. Be strong.

I've seen how John has been pressed, my son is he. I have selected him to be bruised and afflicted and reproached for my name's sake, and he will come to me for refuge. Will I not protect and renew his strength then and encourage him now? For he is one of my selected ones. Hold fast. Thou must not leave until I tell thee. Your time must be my time."

My niece, Beth, found an old diary in a box she was going through that her dad Johnny had given her years ago. The diary was one my mother had written in 1954. Beth thought I might want it. This diary was a great treasure to me and I've chosen to share some of it here.

From the diary of Mary Powell

Friday, Jan. 1, 1954—*Today is sunny and warm, a bit windy. May God soon give Herbert his sight. Marjorie has been here today and washed for herself and me. I hope God ever increases her strength. Ruth's folks were up to see her and it was Caroline's seventh birthday. I'm starting to read the book Under His Wings. I have read over four chapters in the Bible too. I'm going to ask Jesus to help me live more close to Him this year than ever before and open up my spiritual understanding.*

Saturday, Jan. 2—*Today cooler but sunny and pretty. Mae and Marie were here today and said Curtis's brother is pretty sick, and that he had gone to Tennessee. Dad and Herbert and Ruth and Carrol all went to Jackson today. Herbert said his eyes were getting worse all the time. Oh, it makes me feel so bad. But I know God is faithful and sometime Herbert will see again. I've read two chapters in my Bible today. James and Carrol and*

Herbert all went to Waverly church. Brother Morgan was there.

Sunday, Jan. 3—*I read six chapters in the Bible today. Marjorie and John came down and we all had a little service here. We had no way of going to church. Edwin was pretty sick, but God gave us victory. Erby and the boys took a walk. It was such a pretty day.*

Monday, Jan. 4—*Today I only read one chapter in the Bible. I didn't get to sleep until 3:30 am because Timmy is worse and Edwin couldn't move yet. (I mean because of his hips.) But I know he's well for we are trusting God and He will never leave us alone. It's windy, looks like rain or it may snow. Marjorie came down to iron.*

Tuesday, Jan. 5—*Today Marjorie came down and stayed with the children while we went to town. I got Edwin a puzzle game and Herbert got him a gun. He is better but can't use his right leg. He can use the left one pretty well. I read one chapter today in the Bible. I saw Brother Brandenburg in the Kroger store today. I got some pictures of George and his wife today. Oh, how I wish they would both get saved. There's a big snow this morning, started about five am.*

Wednesday, Jan. 6—*Today is Ruth's birthday. It's snowing a little today but not as cold as yesterday. Edwin can use both legs today, but can't walk yet. Thank the Lord for his goodness to us. Wilmer came up and he and Herbert went to his place to cut trees with the power saw. Herbert and Wilmer didn't get back. They had a wreck, and Herbert is in the hospital in Chillicothe. I know God will help him somehow. I read four chapters in the Bible today.*

Thursday, Jan 7—*It sure is nice out today. They want to operate on Herbert but he won't let them. I'm glad. He said he didn't know when he'd get to come home. Ruth, Marjorie, Herbert, Wilmer and Jack all went to see Herbert and he can't see a thing. He can only tell it's daylight. I kept little Mary and Roger today. I read four chapters in the Bible today.*

Friday, Jan. 8—*It sure is pretty again today. Ruth and I and Curtis and Wilmer went to see Herbert today. He's about the same, but won't know until after the doctor comes in on Monday when he can come home. I read one chapter in the*

Bible.

Saturday, Jan. 9—It sure is cold today. I was working about and looked out the window and there was Herbert and some man. I sure was surprised. The doctor told Herbert he'll always be blind. The jolt from the accident had tore the retina clean off above and below and the doctor was glad he hadn't operated. We went to church and Herbert was prayed for. God allowed him to see some. Not clear, but I know someday he will.

Sunday, Jan. 10—A big snow but not too cold. Today I kept Roger while Herbert drove down to Piketon to see Herbert Steffy. Wilmer came back with him. I read three chapters today. This evening Marjorie, John, Calvin, and Armetha all came down and we had church service here.

Monday, Jan. 11—A warmer and pretty day. Herbert and I started to take Wilmer home. The old car went bad. A tie-rod came loose and we had to walk a long way to Frank Steffy's house. Then he took us home. I got a letter from Elisha today. Sure was glad to hear from him. Edwin went to school today.

Tuesday, Jan 12—It's cold again today, but I have to do a big washing. Ruth hung out most of my clothes for me. It sure was a help. I didn't read much in the Bible today. Calvin came down for us to pray for Marjorie. She had a spell with her heart. Herbert, Ruth and their baby didn't feel well either. Marjorie is doing better though weak.

Wednesday, Jan. 13—A cold but fair day. Early today they came after me again to pray for Marjorie. She was much stronger when I left. John took their stove and washer home. I sure do feel bad today. Carrol done the Bible reading tonight for us.

Thursday, Jan 14—It has snowed all day. I coughed until I'm so sore and tired. I don't feel like doing anything. I baked light bread. Erby's gone fox hunting. I kept Edwin home, seems like he's taking a fresh cold again. I read three chapters today in the Bible.

Tuesday, Jan. 19—Today is little Tommy's birthday. He is now in Glory with Jesus, waiting for us to come to him.

Monday, Mar. 1, 1954—We sure did have a snow last night and most of today. It seems like I'm feeling better than I have for some time. I've had the flu for so long and could scarcely walk for a while. The Lord blessed me so good a week ago. I still feel His sweet presence.

Mar. 6—Brother Baxter preached: "What faith takes out, unbelief brings back."

Wednesday, Mar. 17—Special singing congregational. Talk from Brother Baxter. Later a testimony read from a man who had cancer. Another brother gave announcements for their Church of God Tidings Tabernacle. Prayer by congregation was lengthy. Reading by Brother Baxter, Luke chapter five: "Faith cometh by hearing".

Milk and honey flow. Pour out my spirit—plenty of it.

Tuesday, Mar. 23, 1954—Eph 3:12

God gave us promises even when he knew we were unworthy, and wanted us to believe him and accept we have access. Angels are sent forth to serve us and protect us. What God's word says challenges of faith, present conditions, been acted upon by God's word. Five wounds bear prayers for me, which he received upon the Cross.

Wednesday, Mar 24—John 5:14, Heb 3:6, Heb 10:19, Heb 10:35

I am a son. Angels are mine. When I come boldly before the throne with confidence. Genuine prayer must be a product of knowing we should thank and praise and welcome him always. Because he is with us we must accept that which he has already given us.

Thursday, Mar. 25—Do not fling away your fearless trust and confidence in God. Take a word from God. If you abide in me and I in you, you can ask what you will. All the world and hell cannot take it from you. God himself cannot break his word. Should not we then get more of it within our hearts.

Friday, Mar 26—The touch that Jesus feels, who is able to touch him? The earnest sincere petitions, the woman with the bloody issue, the crowd touching him didn't attract his attention.

Saturday, Mar 27—While cleaning house, King Joash finds the last book that was lost. It revives the people.

Sunday, Mar 28—Everything God made is good and pure

for God is love. Everything satan enters, he rules and causes it to be evil and bad. Power of God gives deliverance. Satan makes people steal, kill, drink, etc. But the power of God delivers. Man and doctors cannot set free the devil's captives. Only Jesus. Power of God delivered woman with bloody issue. Doctors failed her. Saul of Tarsus—wisdom and wealth failed him. Angel came to set Peter free from jail. Our confidence and trust in God has great recompense of reward.

Dec. 14-15, 1954—I'm glad I'm a Christian. I'm trusting the Lord. I'm reading my Bible. Believing his Word. The past is forgiven from sin. I'm set free. A mansion in Heaven is waiting for me.

Dec. 31—Comparing Self and Others

God's working things out and not the devil. Don't expect anything good from yourself.

True Science—We must be on the same wavelength as God to get the truth, etc. Our radios and televisions have to be on the right wavelength to get the right station. When Jesus comes he sets the captive free. Jesus was made manifest to destroy Satan. When we just all but touch the hem of his garment, Satan will at once send out the spirit of doubt and fear and weakens us and conquers us. We have to overcome these spirits. Set them where they belong as belonging to Satan and destroy them by faith.

Where is Satan's seat with you?

A man-fearing spirit.

A self-satisfied spirit.

Not concerned about going forward in Godly experiences.

A root of bitterness.

Love waxing cold.

Misplacing our faith by putting it in others instead of Christ the giver.

Forgetting the powerhouse unless something does wrong.

***

My Encounters with Angels

Farmer Powell and his two sons

(A story written for her two youngest sons by Mary E. Powell)

Once upon a time a farmer with his family lived in a pretty, peaceful valley. On either side of the valley the hills came up so pretty, all covered with beautiful green trees. But what was best of all for the farmer's young sons, Johnny and Timmy, was that there was a creek, and in this creek they fished and played most of the time.

One bright summer day Farmer Powell came in for his dinner. As he was eating, he said, "Boys, I'm going to tell you now I found a yellow jackets' nest in some weeds under a tree by the creek. You better stay away from there. Do you hear?"

Of course Johnny and Timmy Powell were quick to answer, "Yes." Just as quick came another thought that got them into trouble. Of course trouble was nothing new for them. For there was the time Johnny had an excellent idea and would show Timmy he could drive Daddy Powell's truck. He got it started all right but couldn't get it stopped. As luck would have it, at the bottom of the driveway there stood Daddy Powell's corncrib. So down the hill went the truck with Johnny at the steering wheel. Into the corncrib he went, knocking it almost off its foundation. Johnny suffered with a whipping, and the boys were sent to bed. The corncrib still sits crooked, reminding us of that experience.

Let's get back to our yellow jackets' nest. These yellow jackets really liked their new home. The creek with its babbling song and cool breezes was so sweet to them, they guarded it well. Two guards were on duty that day. They could hear what Daddy said for one was on the windowsill while the family was eating dinner.

Daddy Powell went back to work in the fields and Mommy Powell was doing dishes. But Johnny and Timmy were preparing themselves for battle.

We'll call these two yellow jacket guards Peep and Boo. Peep said, "Boys, I want you to look coming here. Did you ever see the like?"

All the yellow jackets gathered to look and this is what they saw: Timmy and Johnny coming as brave as a lion sure of its prey. Each boy had their pockets bulging with rocks and a rock in each hand. Sure of conquering their foes with victory written all over their faces.

The yellow jackets held a quick meeting. Peep and Boo told the others to go back to the nest and when he gave the word, to charge.

Peep said he and Boo would watch, and watch they did! Peep said, "I want you to look at Timmy. Look at the joyful grin all over his face. I'll change that for him. Just you wait and see."

Boo said, "Take a look at Johnny. My, how sure he is of himself. Well, I'll change his mind for him."

"Look, they're getting nearer. Boo, go tell the rest to come on and get ready. Oh, ho ho. Watch them draw back that rock, would you? Ok. Ready! Go!"

Zing. Zing. Peep got right under Johnny's arm and stung. Then no one could keep count of all that went on. Rocks flying and yellow jackets soaring.

At the house Mommy Powell heard such screams as you never heard before. She hurried to the door to see what was the matter. She saw two poor little boys. No longer brave or joyful at the thought of victory who ran into her arms. Defeated, swollen and sobbing out their story.

Yes, you guessed it. They were really scolded. But Mommy thought they were punished enough and had learned their lesson well enough.

As for the yellow jackets—they really celebrated their victory. Laughing at the boys who were so much bigger than they were. How they changed their looks and sent them back where they belonged, utterly defeated. Now the yellow jackets feast on clover blooms and refresh themselves in the creek water. Timmy and Johnny stay at their end of the creek. All is well and happy in the little valley again.

By Mary E. Powell

CHAPTER SIXTEEN

My third encounter with an Angel

For it is written, He shall give his angels charge over thee, to keep thee. -Luke 4:10

Every time I had an encounter with an angel it seemed like there was a special place in heaven where God would grant our meeting.

I had taken care of John's mother before she passed away, and then my mother. After making all the arrangements and seeing to all the details for Mom's funeral, I was totally worn down. I tried to go home but passed out as I was getting in the car. John had to turn right around and take me back to the hospital. The doctor said I was exhausted—both physically and emotionally. I ended up spending a week or so in the hospital.

After Mom's death, I asked God to give me something from Him. I felt so empty. I needed to be filled with something more than man could give.

God gave me another vision. It was like he let me slip into heaven where Mom was. My excitement was so great, it was hard for me to grasp each singular detail of the event. Excitement and activity charged the air all around me. The presence of heavenly angels was everywhere. While in heaven, I was escorted by an angel. The angel with me was so big compared to me. I felt enveloped by his love for me. His presence was enormous. Almost more than I could take in. It is so hard to describe in this book. I saw his face, yet I didn't see it.

More than seeing the details of his appearance with my mortal eyes, I felt him. I felt love.

I saw another angel giving each new arrival a shining robe. He was like a serving angel whose purpose was to greet new arrivals. The robe was so gleaming white, it was beyond the white my human eye could process. It was like the glory of the Lord gave them their color and appearance.

Then I saw Mom. She was so beautiful. She looked like she was in her twenties again. Young and vibrant with no sign of sickness or age. Her face was absolutely glowing. I always thought my mother was beautiful, but there, she looked even more beautiful than she ever had on earth. In my spirit I knew this was a special group of people who had labored for the Lord most of their lives and won souls for him.

Those in this group were receiving their robes of righteousness. Even the robes were special. They were white, but it was a special white, unimaginable to the human eye. I thought of when Brother Scott had passed away years earlier. A group of us fell on our knees and began to pray for Brother Scott's family and the grief they were suffering. The Holy Ghost said, "Grieve not, I have already given him his robe of righteousness."

At that moment, I became aware of my daughter, Rebecca, standing beside me. She was about eight-years-old at the time. I thought of her abscessed tooth that needed attention here on earth.

The angel knew what I was thinking. He knew my thoughts and answered them before I knew I wanted an answer. Before I could even form the question for him in my head, I sensed his answer in my spirit. He said, "But here, there is not the slightest defect." Every communication we shared was positive.

Rebecca's presence was there to remind me there will be no defect in heaven. She never complained about the abscessed tooth again.

After that, it was the angel and me again together. Without words, the angel let me know we were getting ready for the Marriage Supper of the Lamb. I was so excited. I thought, "Let me help so we can hurry!"

It seemed like we glided into another area of Paradise. This group was larger than the first. It consisted of people who never had the chance to win anyone for the Lord. There were people who had been aborted as babies or had died in infancy and those who were saved on their deathbeds. They were dressed in white robes with red vests.

The angel sat a little one in front of me so I could help dress him for the Marriage Supper of the Lamb. It was my brother, Tommy, who had died from burns when he was eighteen-months-old. His body was perfect. He didn't have a scar from the fire that killed him. I was so happy to see him. He hadn't done anything for the Lord because he died in infancy, but he was enjoying heaven. My heart swelled with love and praise at the sight of him.

The angel led me into a much larger section of the crowd. This was the largest group I saw. It represented people like the thief on the cross who asked for forgiveness. None of these had won souls for the Lord.

And Jesus said unto him, Verily, I say unto thee, today shalt thou be with me in Paradise. -Luke 23:43

In the larger crowd, I spotted my brother Joseph Carrol. This was the second time I had seen him in a vision since his death. The first time was when Mom and I had the same dream shortly after he died. He was dressed in a different sort of robe than the ones Mom and Tommy wore. Carrol's robe was purple and reminded me of a choir robe. I realized the attire of each group represented the group they belonged to in heaven.

When he saw me, he waved and shouted, "Oh, there's my sis."

He was so happy to see me he could hardly stand still. He was so proud I had souls to offer to the Lord even though he didn't.

I wanted to see more of heaven, but I felt like my time with the angel was up. I was aware of going back to my bed and leaving the Lord's presence.

This vision meant so much to me. I felt the presence of the

Lord for several days afterward. Even when I walked from one room to the other I could sense a nearness that no one else in the house could feel or sense. It was such a comfort like having someone right next to me who understood what I was going through and loved me unconditionally. I didn't share this vision with anyone for a long time. It was a precious moment between the Lord and me.

***

After Mom's death, my youngest brothers, Tim and John, came to live with us. John was twelve and Tim was ten. They were at that age where their greatest delight was teasing girls. I had taken care of Mom and John's mother, and my nerves were on edge. Regardless, we all did our best to get along and get used to living together. Tim and John didn't grow up with sisters since I was their only one, and my girls weren't used to boys in the house.

One day I reached my limit with the teasing and bickering. I told Tim and Johnny not to get the girls screaming anymore. If they did, I was going to spank them. Apparently Tim forgot what I said. He was soon pestering the girls again and getting them upset.

I told him; "Tim, don't you remember what I said?"

"Yes, sis, and I really deserve it!" he said as he took his punishment.

I was really put to the test that day, but I knew I had to follow through with what I said if they were ever going to listen to me. The boys weren't much smaller than me, but I had to make sure the spanking hurt a little.

***

The Glad Game

Years earlier I had heard a story about a missionary and his family in Africa. The church back home tried to send them a box each Christmas. Just simple things they could afford to send. The family had a little girl who was five or six at the time.

My Encounters with Angels

When the family received the box from their home church, they eagerly opened it. They searched through the box, only to find it contained nothing for the little girl.

At the very bottom, they found a crutch.

The little girl's daddy said, "Let's play the Glad Game. No matter what happens we will find something to be glad about. The harder we have to look for something to be glad about, the better the Glad Game will work."

The little girl thought for a while and then said, "I guess I can be glad I don't have to use the crutch."

I taught the Glad Game to my girls. After Tim and Johnny came to live with us, I taught the Glad Game to them too.

One year over Christmas break, the Robersons asked to take Rebecca with them to Tennessee where they were holding a revival so she could sing to the congregation. Tim wanted to go too. Rebecca knew how much he wanted to go so she asked the Robersons if he could go with them. They finally gave in and let Tim go.

Tim was so excited. The very first night in Tennessee he went with the boys to bring in the cows to milk. There were woods and cliffs in the area where the family was staying. Tim was an outdoorsman like his father. He ventured out exploring, anxious to see what the area had to offer. Soon he came upon a huge cliff with a grapevine hanging out over it. Just the thing he needed to play Tarzan. He grabbed hold of the vine and stepped back as far as the vine would reach. Then he made a run for it yelling the Tarzan call as he went. He lofted out over the edge of the cliff. Then came the unmistakable sound of branches breaking. Tim found himself dropping, dropping over the side of the cliff. He landed at the bottom of the embankment. The pain in his leg was excruciating. The yell he gave that time wasn't the Tarzan yell. Rescuers had quite a job getting Tim up the face of the cliff and to the hospital.

He spent the remainder of the trip laid up. The pastor's wife had to stay at the house with him the whole time.

When he got home, he told me while he was on his back thinking of his busted leg and all the fun he wasn't having, he kept thinking about the Glad Game. Even though it wasn't the trip he had envisioned, it didn't take long to find something to be glad about. He said he sure was glad he hadn't broken both legs. Rebecca became his main servant, along with the rest of the family, until his cast came off.

> For he said, Surely they are my people, children that will not lie; so he was their Savior. ~Isaiah 63:8

***

John's sister-in-law raised chickens and sold eggs from their farm in Carmel. The kids loved to go out behind the chicken house to play. One evening I was getting supper ready before John came home from work.

Tim and Johnny had been out behind the chicken house for a long time. When they finally came to the house to get ready for supper I smelled cigarette smoke. My heart sank. I wondered where I had gone wrong with them.

I asked them if they had been smoking. They had never lied to me before, and I hoped they wouldn't now. They said, "We found a pack of cigarettes, so we tried them."

I know they thought I would yell at them and punish them. Instead I went straight to the bedroom and knelt down next to the bed. My heart felt like it was breaking. I cried and cried. I didn't know what else I could do. I didn't think I could take anymore.

It wasn't long before one of the boys came in and put his hand on my back. He started crying with me. Then the other one came in and did the same thing. They assured me they'd never smoke cigarettes again. They didn't as long as they lived with us. God took care of the situation for me.

John Bradley Powell

David Timothy Powell

Red Shouting Shoes

I remember one time when John was serving as pastor at the church in Carmel I really needed a pair of dress shoes for church. I went to Hillsboro to see what I could find. Like everything else on me, my feet were very small. I wore a size 4.5 shoe, and they were always hard to find. Finally I found a pair with a small heel that fit perfectly, but they were red. In those days, women didn't wear red to church, especially pastor's wives. Maybe that's why I wasn't particularly fond of the color. But they sure were pretty, and I couldn't ask for a nicer fit. I tried them on one last time as I tried to make my decision.

The Lord spoke to me, "You will shout in those shoes."

My decision made, I bought the shoes. I called them my 'shouting red shoes'. The Lord was right, of course. I shouted in those shoes many times.

CHAPTER SEVENTEEN

Building a Church

In the early 1960's we were living in Carmel. John believed his work was done at the Carmel Church of God. The church had been established, and we were ready to move on.

May Hush and Girlie Newberry, two beloved sisters in the Lord, came to our house and said they were starving. Of course they meant spiritually starving. They had been visiting big churches in the area, but they weren't being fed spiritually. They believed the Lord wanted us to have another church closer to them in Hillsboro.

John and I started praying about building a Pentecostal church in Hillsboro. One of the sisters had a dream that confirmed our belief to build the church. We prayed until we prayed through, knowing this was what the Lord wanted us to do.

John said, "If I don't build it now, it won't be built."

In 1964, May Hush, Girlie Newberry, and I shoveled our first shovel full of dirt to build the first Church of God in Hillsboro, Ohio. We all knew we were in God's will, and he would honor our service to him.

May and Girlie stuck with us through thick and thin. John and I mortgaged everything to build this church. We knew God was doing the directing, and we wanted to obey him in every way.

John was working at a foundry in Xenia at the time. It was

at that time, he first started having serious health problems. We suspected he had his first heart attack when we lost our son Tommy, though we never knew for sure. Those health problems never went away completely, and now they seemed to plague him worse than ever. He suffered often from weakness and shortness of breath. Sometime he would get really bad and cough up black phlegm.

Through it all, he didn't complain. He would drive home to Carmel every evening to eat dinner and then go into town to the church and work until it was too dark to work anymore.

My brother Tim was still living with us. He worked a lot on the church too. John bought a tent from a friend of ours named Otis Ramsey. The tent had holes in it, but John figured a tent with holes was better than no tent at all.

The men decided to erect the tent so we could start having services right away. John built a platform and a podium. One night a bad storm tore through town and blew the tent down. Only one tent stake remained to keep the tent from blowing completely away.

The wind even blew over the old upright piano my Aunt Marie had donated to the church. It rang out a melody as it fell over. We believed God was just hurrying us along so we would finish the building faster.

We didn't focus on any negative part of the process. Our hearts rejoiced at the progress we were making. Sister Hush bought blocks for the building of the sanctuary. John spent every spare minute at the church site, working hard and praying for God's blessings to be upon us. Different members of the congregation donated their time and work. It was really appreciated.

Finally our labors paid off. The big day arrived on a beautiful sunny Easter Sunday. That seemed like the perfect day to dedicate our church. It was like the glory of the Lord just came down and filled our little humble church we had dedicated to him. As I sat in my seat and looked around the room, the walls shone like diamonds to me.

There was a hundred or so people present during that first service. What rejoicing there was. Some even hated to go home!

Many of the precious saints that worshipped with us at the church have gone on to be with the Lord. There was much yet to be added, but God continued to supply every need.

Groundbreaking of the Hillsboro Church of God. From left; Girlie Newberry, Marjorie Reed, May Hush.

John and Marjorie in front of the completed church at 621 South East Street in Hillsboro. Painting over Marjorie's shoulder was done by local artist, Truby Abbott.

We were so honored to have a local artist agree to paint the picture on the front of our church. Truby Abbott was born and raised in the hills of Blue Creek, Ohio. When he was in school, Truby often had visions of painting backdrops in church baptisteries.

When he was seventeen or eighteen, Truby gave his heart to the Lord. He was the first person in his family to get saved. By living out his faith every day, Truby won his mom and dad to the Lord.

At Christmastime in 1944, Truby noticed a beginners' Acme paint set and bought it. He told his wife Zetta she could give it to him for his Christmas present that year. Truby was excited to get started. He tried to mix the oil colors together but found he just couldn't paint. He sat at his old writing desk and bowed his head. He asked the Lord to help him paint. He told God he would use his talent for God's glory, and he would tell everyone God had given him the gift to paint.

John and Truby knew each other since they were both pastors and evangelists. John asked Truby if he could paint a mural in the front of our church of Jesus being baptized. He also asked for one on the large window in front of the church of Jesus with his hands raised toward heaven. The paintings were both life sized and beautifully done. We couldn't be happier with the finished products.

Truby has done other paintings all over the United States, as well as some foreign countries. He also did signs for businesses and individuals. The Abbott sign company continues in Hillsboro and Wilmington through Truby's son Randy and his grandsons. I want to thank his daughter Sharon for talking with me and sharing some things about Truby, his gifts, and his love for the Lord.

> *And it shall come to pass afterward, that I will pour out my spirit upon all flesh; and your sons and your daughters shall prophesy, your old men shall dream dreams, your young men shall see visions.* -Joel 2:28

***

I'm sure our girls remember the time their daddy fell and broke the bones in one of his legs. He was helping John Newberry replace the roof on a building at the Newberry farm. That morning John slipped on a frosty board. Not only did he break the bones in his leg, he also sat down on the leg as he was falling, and the leg turned completely around behind him.

That morning I hadn't wanted John to go to work. I wanted him to stay home and spend the day with me. We had so little time together. As he was going out the door, I kissed him goodbye and told him teasingly not to fall and break a leg.

Later when John Newberry called and told me John had fallen and broken his leg, I thought he was kidding. I couldn't believe it actually happened. Somehow John Newberry was able to fashion a makeshift splint out of a board to straighten John's leg enough to get him into the back of his truck and take him to the hospital in Hillsboro. The doctor didn't put any pins in John's leg, and it was always crooked as a result.

Our daughter, Mary, was working at the Highland District Hospital at the time and helped take care of her dad.

John's injuries kept him laid up for a long time, but it didn't keep him from fulfilling his duties at the church. Even though his leg was broken and set in a full cast, he went to church and preached every time he was able. He had to sit in a chair in front of the pulpit, but that didn't slow him down. His burning desire to preach God's word had not diminished.

On the Sundays John wasn't able to preach, I filled in for him. I was thankful for the opportunity to help take the burden off John. Not to mention, I enjoyed sharing my love for the Lord with our church family.

All through his life John loved the old song by The Goodmans: *"I Don't Regret One Mile."*

One day I asked John if he should go first, what did he want to be remembered for the most. Without any hesitation, he said, "I want to be remembered for giving God my all, and for the church." We are so glad we gave God our best years and obeyed his will in every way we knew how.

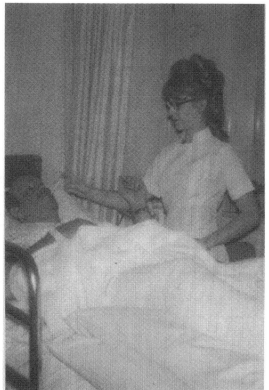

John recovering from his broken leg at the Highland District Hospital. Nurse pictured with him is daughter Mary Reed.

Going over my prayers

When Tim graduated from Sinking Springs High School, I was so proud of him. Unfortunately, I was too sick to go to his graduation. I was disappointed I couldn't be there for his big day. John had helped him get his first car. He and his buddies went out the night they graduated and totaled the car. John said he wouldn't help Tim get another car.

Like several of my other brothers, Tim decided to enlist in the Army. Before he left, I had a talk with him. I said, "I want to tell you one thing before you go. When you are tempted to drink, I want you to know you'll have to go over my prayers to do it."

After Tim got home from the Army, he told me I would never know how many times those words came to him when he drank.

A Surprise Baby

One Sunday evening before the church service was to begin, I noticed a little elderly lady come into the church with something wrapped in a baby blanket. She quietly sat down in a pew. I was curious to see the baby in her arms. I went over to her and asked if I could see her baby. She hesitated a moment before she pulled back a corner of the blanket where the baby's head should be. My mouth flew open though I was too shocked to make a sound. Inside the blanket was a little Chihuahua dog.

I sure was surprised. Sometimes people would carry doll babies in their arms like they were real babies. But this was certainly the first time we had a dog inside the church during our service. How would the dog react? What would the congregation do if they knew we had a dog in church? I didn't know what to do.

The little lady looked up at me. Her eyes so sincere as she promised the dog would not disturb the service in any way. Church was about to begin. I had to get back to my seat. I still didn't know what to do. I took a deep breath and hurried up front to my seat. I didn't say a word about it to John. I figured I would just wait and see what would happen. I would find out the same time as everyone else. To my surprise and wonder, the dog never made a sound. The lady brought her *baby* back to church several times.

Moving

It was soon time to move from Carmel to Hillsboro. John's leg was still in a cast, and he was unable to go with me to look for houses. One morning we sat at the kitchen table and made a list of the things we wanted our new home to have. The first thing on the list was a front porch. We knew we would probably grow old in whatever house we chose, and I had always dreamed of sitting on a front porch with John watching the neighborhood children play and waiting for our own grandchildren to come visit. To me, a house just wasn't a home without a front porch.

We also wanted a living room with a fireplace, a dining room, three bedrooms with one of them upstairs, a roomy kitchen with plenty of cabinets, a basement, and of course a bathroom.

That day I prayed for God to direct me to the right house, one that suited all our wants and needs and was within our budget.

With a prayer in my heart, and quite a bit of excitement about what the day would bring, I ventured out with our daughter, Mary, to begin our search. We looked at several houses I had seen listed in the newspaper, but none of them seemed right. Then we went to Muntz Street to look at another listing. I knew that house wasn't right for us either, but we looked through it anyway. As we were climbing back into the car, Mary noticed a house down the street with a For Sale sign in the front yard.

"What do you think of that one, Mom?" she asked.

I shrugged. I was a little tired of looking, but so far I hadn't been satisfied with any of the other houses we looked at. "It won't hurt to look," I told her, though I didn't have very high hopes.

As we opened the front door, the Spirit of the Lord spoke to me. "This is your home."

I loved it from the start. How could I not? We looked around, and I saw it had all the things I had asked the Lord for. Naturally there were a few issues that would need redone. The porch had a few loose boards. I immediately recognized that a concrete floor would be better anyway. I could already imagine a swing with John and me holding hands and swinging happily in it.

The house even included a bonus from the Lord I hadn't thought to put on my list: a carport so John would have somewhere to park the car.

There was no need to look any further. I was so excited I

could hardly wait to get home to tell John about the house we found. John was already asleep when Mary and I got home that evening. I woke him up so he'd be wide awake when I told him I had found our new home that day.

He wasn't as excited as I expected him to be. I guess he was a doubting Thomas. After I told him all the details, he said, "I don't reckon," as if he couldn't believe our search had ended so soon.

I swallowed my impatience. "John, I know I found the house God has for us."

I started telling him how the rooms were laid out and all the potential I saw in the house. I told him how it had all the things on our list. The more I talked, the more excited I got all over again.

I grabbed his hand. "Let's go. Mary and I will take you to see it right now and you'll see for yourself I'm right."

John still wasn't excited. He shook his head. "They probably want too much money."

I swallowed another sigh. I knew he'd come around, especially after he saw the house for himself. I also knew God would work out all the details about financing and making whatever improvements the house needed. Most of all, I knew God would give my husband the same vision he'd already placed in me.

I was so excited I could hardly sleep. I wrote many pages in my diary that night about the house and how God had answered my prayers so quickly. I didn't stop talking about it until John agreed to go see the house with me.

A few days later we drove to see the cute little house on the end of Muntz Street in Hillsboro. As we pulled into the driveway, I could see John was looking everything over and pondering the decision in his mind. He was surprised to learn the Davis family owned the house. They were building a new home at nearby Rocky Fork Lake. They had gone to church with us years ago, and we knew they were good people. I think that brought John some peace about the situation.

John went through the house room by room. I wondered if he was looking for something wrong with it. After he came back upstairs from the basement, he said we probably needed to have a talk with the Davises. My heart soared. I knew what that meant.

As I already knew, the price was perfect for our budget. After selling our house in Carmel, we would have enough left over to install a furnace and later replace the wooden floor on the front porch with a good concrete one.

Mary and Rebecca were the only girls still living at home at this point. They were so excited to be moving into town. The biggest decision for them was deciding who would get which room upstairs.

I think we three girls were more excited about moving than John was. It was all we could talk about. The next few weeks were very busy, packing and planning, and making all the final decisions necessary when selling one house and moving into another. The Davises were still moving out of the house on Muntz Street, so that added a lot of confusion as we prepared to move in.

We had some special friends from our church, Evelyn and Ernie Brewer, to help us. Evelyn was the one who was scared of the groundhogs at our house on Roundhead Road. Ernie was a very comical person. He was always pulling pranks on people. You never could tell when he was telling the truth or when he was kidding around.

Ernie loved to dress up like Santa Claus at Christmas, and he and John would take treats and small gifts to area nursing homes. John always made sure the widows in the church had a little money at Christmas.

My Encounters with Angels

Ernie Brewer dressed as Santa, pictured with Reed daughters from left; Mary, Lois, Leona, Rebecca

Evelyn and Ernie were a big help to us during our move to town. After days of hard work, we finally got down to the last trip from Carmel to our new home on Muntz Street. Ernie had been a big help to Mary. John couldn't do much because of his broken leg, and I was too busy unpacking and organizing every carload they delivered to the new house. The last things Mary and Ernie loaded into the car were John and the dog. Mary and Ernie were exhausted. It had been a really long day.

Ernie rode in the backseat with the dog. They hadn't driven far when Ernie told Mary the dog had thrown up on him. She couldn't tell if he was telling the truth or not since he was always teasing about something. Then the telltale odor of dog vomit reached her nose. There was no doubt this time he was telling the truth. She couldn't keep from laughing though John told her to stop. Later when Mary wasn't around, John told me he had been dying to laugh himself, but he didn't want to hurt Ernie's feelings. When we went to bed that night, he started thinking about it again and began heehawing and laughing so hard the whole bed shook.

The only member of the family who wasn't happy about the move to Muntz Street was the dog. He was an outside country dog and couldn't acclimate to life in town. He kept running down to the neighbor's house on the corner. The neighbor, Jesse, was the uncle of one of the ladies in our church. He whistled all the time. Maybe that's why the dog liked him. Whatever the reason, we always found the dog at Jesse's house after he'd run off. Finally we let him stay there and everybody was happy.

***

Our new house had an oil stove in the dining room that we relied on for heat while we waited for the installation of our new furnace. One morning shortly after we moved in I tried to light the oil furnace. We had used it before so I didn't expect a problem, but for some reason I couldn't get it to light that day.

I called for John to come and see if he could figure out what was wrong. It didn't take much investigating for him to realize soot had built up over the years and was hanging all over the inside of the stove. We knew that meant a long, messy cleanup. John got the sweeper and went to work cleaning out the soot.

Suddenly a loud bang reverberated through the room. I screamed as the sweeper bag exploded. A huge black cloud filled the room and enveloped both of us. John and I couldn't even see each other.

What a mess! As the cloud dissipated, all we could see were the whites of each other's eyes. I couldn't decide if I wanted to laugh or cry. I thought of all the work it would take to clean ourselves and the room and the rest of the house as black soot settled into every crack and vent. John looked at me. I looked at him. Then we started laughing at the same time. I guess in a situation like that you might as well laugh. There was nothing wrong a lot of soap and water and hard work wouldn't fix.

We sure had a mess. We worked on each other first, cleaning the black dust off our clothes, our hair, our skin, even the insides of our noses and our ears. Then we tackled the house. But we were determined to have a pretty house. God had blessed us with so much, and we wanted it to be nice.

I don't think we worked harder in our lives than we did that day. With our goal pressing us onward, we made it. One of the best things about our new home was its close proximity to our church. Being on Muntz Street made it much easier for us to work on the church and to worship with our church family. Things were moving forward. We were so excited about the direction the Lord was leading.

John got a job working in construction with Vern Coss. Vern was always willing to give advice to John while they built the church. Vern and John also got contracts to work on the post office in Hillsboro, the Dayton Mall, and other projects.

Rocky Coss, Vern's son, would hitch a ride with the men on their way to a worksite in the morning so they could drop him off at the college where he was attending law school. Now Rocky is a judge in Hillsboro. We are very proud of him. Vern's younger daughter, Dorrie, loved to play checkers with John. She was such a sweet thing. She would laugh and tease John every time she beat him. Another daughter, Melody, had such a beautiful smile. She meant so much to us. She is now married to Greg James, and both of them have been so supportive of John and me and to our church over the years.

While working on our house, John's health began to grow worse. A dear brother at the church, Wilbur Fronk, had a son-in-law who came to preach sometimes when John wasn't feeling up to it. The son-in-law's name was John Maggard, and my, he was on fire for the Lord.

John Maggard was a very down-to-earth person from southern Kentucky. He hadn't been brought up in the church like the rest of us, so he sure was different. He loved to tell stories of growing up as a poor man in Kentucky. His stories were so funny. He used to say his family was so poor, but at least they had running water. They just had to run a mile to get it. We loved spending time with him.

Over the next few years, we realized John would soon have to retire from preaching. His doctors said he could no longer take the strain of full time work. The congregation had heard John Maggard preach a few revivals and special services for us, and they really liked him. When it came time for John to retire, the Church of God began looking for his replacement and finally decided John Maggard would be the new pastor.

Years later, I learned John Maggard's wife Pat had been very concerned about coming to Hillsboro. On the drive for their first service, she told him; "How will they accept me? I'll never fill Sister Reed's shoes." I was honored and humbled that she believed I was a suitable role model for her. She and I became such good friends, and she filled her role as pastor's wife in a way that honored the Lord and honored our church.

CHAPTER EIGHTEEN

Some of the founding members of the Hillsboro church

special member of our church family I want to mention is Wilbur Fronk. He is the one who introduced us to his son-in-law John Maggard who later became our pastor. Brother and Sister Fronk were always very kind to our family. When Wilbur went to the grocery store and found things on sale, he would buy extra and bring a whole box of groceries to our door. He wasn't one to do things to be seen so he did this privately. We felt so much love from him and his wife. They are both in glory now.

Pastor John Maggard and his wife Pat were always so special to us. There are many special things they have done for us through the years. When we had our sixtieth wedding anniversary they sent the choir from our church to sing and play for us in our yard on Muntz Street.

The song that stood out to me most was when Keith Crothers, the youth director, Missy Taylor, and Darnella Williamson led the choir in, *The Anchor Holds*. That's just how John and I felt. We knew God's presence was surrounding us in a special way. It was a very memorable day for us. Steve Hertenstein also came with them. He has always been so helpful with the youth at our church. We appreciate everything he does. As they sang *The Anchor Holds* I saw tears rolling down our daughter Lois's cheeks. I'm not sure if she was touched by the song or what the church had done in honor of our anniversary.

Another time the church surprised us with a special service

to honor us. They entitled the service, *This is your life*. There were visitors from some of the churches we pastored over the years. Many spoke of our acquaintance and the influence John and I had on their lives. It really showed us their love.

John and Marjorie pictured with Reverend John and Pat Maggard

I'm pretty sure Sister Unia Faye Williams had a lot to do with many of the special services at the church. She and her husband Darrell have always been such a blessing to the church over the years. Their singing has blessed me in so many ways. They had just celebrated their fiftieth wedding anniversary at the time of our special service. Two of their children, Darrell Junior and Darnella are a light and a blessing. We love and appreciate their entire family. They have filled many positions in the church.

There are many other precious members of the church who have contributed to our lives. I cannot mention them all. God called Pastor John Maggard home in August of 2012. What a reunion Pastor Maggard and John must have had. Bishop Dan Hess and his wife Lisa were pastors for a while. They were very supportive of me as I started work on this book. They visited and prayed with us, and it meant so much. Due to health reasons Pastor Hess resigned. Now Reverend and Mrs. John Coyle are our shepherds, and we pray God's blessings upon them.

There were many special people at the Hillsboro Church of God who have helped our family and meant a lot to me. Sister

Gracie Johnson wrote me the following poem. She is a dear sister in the Lord to me.

We need water to drink.
To wash dishes in the sink.
To take a bath and mop the floor,
My, it's good for so much more.
Hope you are feeling better and truly on the mend.
God loves you and I do, too, because you are a special friend.
I would send you the sun if I could, but it is fixed for all to see,
　The clouds cover it for a time for we need rain and snow so the crops will grow.
Waterfalls are beautiful, it's nice to watch them flow.
From the stream to the river and then to the sea,
Water means a lot to you and me.
God made everything good.
Sometimes man is the necessary evil in his plan.

By Gracie McCane Johnson
January 12, 2004

***

Beverly and Tim McKeever and their family were faithful to support us and the church over the years. Altogether, there have been five generations from Beverly's family that helped us build the church.

One member of her family is a dear sister I watched grow up in the church. I remember when Melissa Hammitt was just a baby and would come to church. She has been such a blessing to me, especially over the last few years. She would stop to visit and bring me something to eat. She would soak my feet and do other kind and thoughtful things for me. When my precious little fourteen-year-old dog Princess died, Melissa and Mary took care of the situation for me. Melissa has been like an angel to me. She even played a part in completing this book when she brought Teresa Slack into the project.

Other dear friends of ours were Brother and Sister Mechley. They asked if they could tithe by cleaning the church. We were delighted and so blessed by their sacrifice. While cleaning the church, they would anoint each pew and pray for the congregation. Their service was always done with such love. They passed away within a few hours of each other, and a double funeral was held for them at the church. Now they are in heaven receiving their reward.

I will always remember the Roach family who came to our church playing music and singing so beautifully for the congregation. It lifted up the Lord and we all rejoiced with them.

The Mannings were another wonderful family who sang and played the piano for us. Their daughter Christine hopped all over the stool and even the keys when she played. She used to call me her adopted mom. The family eventually moved to California and we all missed them.

John and I met Russell and Virginia Moore and their sons at a church in Harveysburg where Brother Rader was the pastor. Of course you remember Brother Rader was the one who married John and me in 1948. Over the years, we became very close friends with the Moore family. Our girls and their boys became friends too. Many good times were shared at our house.

One of my favorite songs Brother and Sister Moore sang for the Lord was, "I Just Steal Away Somewhere". Their singing and Brother Moore's guitar playing was so anointed. Their son Tom became an anointed singer as well. John always said Tom was one of his favorite gospel singers.

Years later, Brother Moore told us he still remembered John's sermon from that night in Harveysburg. Sister Moore was a wonderful cook. All the Moore sons would jump right in to help any time work needed done at the church.

Sister Coomer was a faithful sister in the Lord in all her ways. Her heart's desire was to see her husband saved. She prayed for him for more than forty years. She was so precious and dedicated. She was there the night her husband prayed through to salvation. I was sick that night and wasn't able to see it. But I am forever thankful Sister Coomer lived to see her prayers answered.

Kenneth and Elsie Rankin were also there in our early days at the Hillsboro church. They were so faithful to the church. Brother Rankin was very polite and reserved. Every time we had a dinner Sister Rankin made the best fried chicken. We visited their house several times over the years. Mary was fascinated by their daughter Karen's bedroom, which she thought was decorated like a princess room. That's what she remembers best about the Rankins' home.

Brother Clarence Freeland attended church with his grandson Darrell. Brother Freeland would sing with Evelyn Brewer. Their voices harmonized so beautifully together. Darrell wanted to sing by himself. He would tell everyone what page to turn to in the red hymnals we used. Darrell is a faithful prayer warrior for me to this day.

Lucille Howard was another dedicated member of our congregation. She attended faithfully and always brought her five children with her. There was Gene, Shirley, K.G., Ronnie, and Louise. Her kids were very dedicated to her. You could see how much they loved and honored her. It was a testament to what a wonderful woman she was.

Sometimes the church's teenagers would come to our home to visit and sing for us. It always meant so much to John and me. As we watched them, my thoughts would drift to each one of them, and I would wonder what God had planned for their lives. Tom Dalton's voice always rang out in songs and lifted my spirits so much. His family travels and sings for the Lord now.

Another person who has lifted my spirits over the years is Becky Norman. I watched Becky grow up in the church. Her parents were our choir directors for many years. Becky started teaching Children's Church when she was practically a kid herself. She has blossomed into a beautiful woman, wife, mother, and sister in the Lord. She is always willing to pitch in any time the church or someone in her church family has a need.

God knew what we needed when the Felson family joined our church. Sister Felson was a dedicated prayer warrior. We could depend on her praying for all situations until God moved.

We will always cherish our memories of Evelyn and Ernie Brewer. Evelyn was our songbird. She taught our littlest members, who loved her very much. Her students still give her praise today, so may we all let our light shine for our heavenly father. She was so multi-talented and helped us in many ways. Ernie kept us laughing, always seeing the funny side of things.

Evelyn and Nolan Zornes have been very good examples of Christian parents for our congregation. God blessed Evelyn with a kind spirit and love to counsel others. She would always say, "We don't talk about people. We pray for them."

The Zornes family has always been special to us. The first time I held their son Kim in my arms in church, I knew God was going to use him in a special way. I didn't tell anyone, but I knew it. Kim always said he wanted to be a preacher like Brother Reed. Watching them grow up was such a joy to us. Both of the Zornes' sons, Kim and Dale, became ministers. God is moving in their lives, and it is wonderful.

I have sat under Dale Zornes's teachings. He brings out the word of God so wonderfully, I enjoy every minute of it. His wife Elisa is very talented. She plays the piano and sings for the glory of God.

Jane Eidenier and her children were very faithful members of our church. Jane's daughter Linda grew up and married Kim Zornes. I remember Linda when she was just a little girl coming to church. God knew her destiny as a pastor's wife and has placed a song and gift of knowledge in her heart.

It would be impossible to write about all the precious saints who have touched our lives through the years. Just know we love you all and cherish our time spent on earth with each of you. What a blessed meeting we will all have someday in Glory.

Do you remember this song?

What a day that will be when my Jesus I shall see. When we look upon his face, the one who saved me by his grace. And when he takes me by the hand and leads me to the promised land. What a glorious day that will be...

"See you there!"

I thank God, whom I serve from my forefathers with pure consciences that without ceasing I have remembrance of thee in my prayers night and day.
-II Timothy 1:2

The Reeds with their dear friends, the Zornes.
Pictured from left: Leona Huddleston, Rebecca Larsen, Mary Reed, John and Marjorie Reed, Linda and Kim Zornes.

Marjorie J. Reed

CHAPTER NINETEEN

Retirement Years

fter John retired, the State Overseer of the Church of God told us it was never a good idea for the former pastor to sit under a new pastor. Sometimes the former pastor had a hard time adjusting to his new position on the pew while the new pastor often found it intimidating to lead the old pastor. John and I prayed about the situation and believed it was best to distance ourselves from the church in Hillsboro so we wouldn't be stepping on the toes of the new pastor. After John got to where he couldn't hold a job, the Lord saw fit to send us to Florida.

One Christmas several years after we moved to Muntz Street, we had to take our youngest daughter Rebecca and her boyfriend Mike, who would later become our son-in-law, back to Lee College in Tennessee where they were both students. While on our way there, we stopped in Kentucky to visit our daughter, Leona, and her husband Jim. We didn't get to see Leona and Jim nearly as much as we wanted since they lived so far away, so we took advantage of every opportunity to work out a visit. We always had such good times when we were together.

That winter was a very cold one. All the water lines on Leona and Jim's farm had frozen. The Lord helped the guys get the pipes open, and the water flowing again. Before the day was over, though, it began snowing again. We figured we needed to get on the road so we could return Rebecca and Mike to Lee College, and John and I could head to the safety of home.

The farther we went, the more treacherous the roads became. We saw jack-knifed semis on the mountain roads and several accidents. After dropping Rebecca and Mike off at school, John and I talked about the nasty weather and dangerous roads. We were seriously concerned about whether we could make it over the mountains to return to Ohio.

We decided to head south where the sun was shining. The thought of warm weather and ocean breezes made me anxious to get out of the mountains. My aunt Marie Powell wintered in Florida and had a nice home there. We had never been to Florida, and it had been so long since John and I got away from home without one of the girls with us, we thought now was as good a time as any. Anticipation and excitement filled my heart. It felt like a whole new chapter of our lives was about to begin. It would start with a brand new honeymoon.

Saint Simons Island

On our way to Florida John and I spotted a sign for St. Simons Island. It sounded lovely and really grabbed our attention. We were feeling adventurous and decided to follow the signs to see St. Simons Island for ourselves. That was my biggest thrill. When I was a kid and first learned there was such a thing as lighthouses, they fascinated me. I hoped I would someday see one, though it didn't seem likely in my southern Ohio home. Though I didn't see a way, God granted me that desire.

The area was so peaceful. John and I just loved it. We visited the park, but the lighthouse was closed so we were only able to admire it from the outside.

We decided to stay overnight in one of the cabins on Saint Simon's Island. All the other tourists were gone since vacation season was over. We had the whole island to ourselves.

That evening we went out to the beach to watch the sunset. We stood in the sifting sand to watch the sun sink over the ocean waves. No sunset had ever been more beautiful to me. Now I was inspired to get up early the next morning to watch the sunrise before we left.

The seagulls were up fishing for breakfast before dawn. As John and I stood on the beach watching the sun come up, the waves seemed to be waving goodbye to us. We hugged each other and kissed. It was like a honeymoon all over again. Watching the sun that morning reminded me of a song John and I would sing at church, *Beyond the Sunset*.

Beyond the sunset, oh, blissful morning,
When with our Savior, heaven is begun.
Earth's toiling ended, oh, glorious dawning.
Beyond the sunset when day is done.

After we left St. Simon's Island, we headed to Aunt Marie's house. It was such a beautiful day. The sun was shining, and it was so warm, we no longer needed our coats. It was quite a change from what we left behind with the kids in Tennessee.

When we arrived at Aunt Marie's, there was no one home. We couldn't believe it. We knocked on the door, but sure enough, no one was there. We were so disappointed. What if they were out of town? What if we had come all this way for nothing? But we were here. There was no point in worrying. We got out of the car and sat on the porch to wait.

Finally Aunt Marie, her sister Ruth, and Uncle Mack got home. They couldn't believe their eyes when we came off the porch to meet them. Mack let out one of his war whoops at the sight of us. It was a fun reunion and special surprise for all of us. They immediately invited us to spend the night, which we knew they would.

It was so nice waking up the next morning to sunshine and warm temperatures instead of snow and icy roads. John wanted to take me for a walk around the neighborhood. I didn't know what to expect when he said he wanted to show me some properties he and Uncle Mack had checked out the night before. Uncle Mack knew the people who owned one of the properties for sale and knew it was a good deal.

To me, the property looked like a jungle. I had never thought about buying a jungle before, but the more John and I looked around, we felt really good about it. We believed the

Lord would work it out so we could buy our jungle. Uncle Mack and Aunt Marie were excited as well and wanted us to have the property.

Aunt Marie told us if we wanted to buy it she would lend us the money. Everything looked like it was falling into place. Feeling that God was giving us the go-ahead, we called the owners and bought the property with much joy. John and I couldn't believe it. To think we were buying a piece of paradise during our very first trip to Florida. It was amazing, like a dream come true. Everything fell effortlessly into place since it was God's will that had led us to Florida.

John and I were alone for the first time in our married life now that the girls were grown and married. We lost no time filling out the proper paperwork with our names in all the right places. We had to chop down trees, clear away brush and grapevines. You name it, it was in our jungle. The first thing we did was have a well dug for water. Some of our new neighbors came over to help. Everyone was friendly and helpful. Thank the Lord for good neighbors.

We lived the first winter on our property in a little truck-bed camper. Mary had painted a picture of the Road Runner from the cartoons on the truck cab. Everyone who saw it thought it was so cute. She had turned into quite an artist. I was so pleased she was creative and talented like her Grandma Mary and the rest of the Steffy family.

John and I knew we needed to keep our eyes open for something else to live in. Our camper was becoming too cramped. We needed more space. John heard about a trailer up the street in our neighborhood that was for sale. He went to talk to the owner to see what we could work out. After seeking the Lord, we decided to buy the trailer. We were so happy the day that trailer rolled onto our lot. Wouldn't you know it? There went another one of Uncle Mack's war whoops.

Silver Springs

One of Aunt Marie and Uncle Mack's favorite places to visit was Silver Springs. They went there every chance they got. They told John and me about the springs that bubbled up through the white sand at the bottom of the lake and how the water was crystal clear. They told us of so many beautiful things there. We thought my dad Erby would like to see it if we ever got him to visit us in Florida.

When I was a little girl and our family lived along the Little Miami River, Dad used to put a trout line across the river from one side to the other to catch fish. Dad was a born fisherman. He always caught lots of fish, snakes, and turtles on that trout line.

One day Dad saw he had caught a huge turtle as big around as a washtub. People came from all over the area to see the turtle. Uncle Arra started calling Dad 'Turtle'. I remember Dad telling us not to put our hands in the water where he kept the turtle because it would bite our hands off.

Dad was so excited when we took him to Silver Springs to see the sea turtles. It made him think of the huge turtle he had caught on the Little Miami River. I was glad Dad got a chance to see the sea turtles during his visit because it was the only time he was able to go to Florida.

While he was there, he loved to sit on our little front porch and eat kumquats he'd gathered from the tree in our yard. Dad loved to watch people and talk to them as they passed by our house. Our little dog, Cindy, which we had gotten to give to Sister Newberry, stayed outside with Dad to keep him company. I guess the outdoorsman/hunter instinct was still alive and well inside of Dad. When a person walked by, he would whistle and sic Cindy on them. That was a go-getter for Cindy, but when John caught her and Dad giving the neighbors grief, he made them stop.

We were surprised that some places in Florida would turn horses loose into their orange groves to let them eat the oranges that were unmarketable. We could hardly believe our eyes whenever we saw it.

My Encounters with Angels

Silver Springs soon became one of our favorite places to visit while we were in Florida. While we were there, we ate alligator tail for the first--and last--time. The restaurant served many other delicacies, but alligator tail wasn't one I liked. It left an awful taste in my mouth that entire day. I kept eating other things, trying to get rid of the taste. Nothing worked. I never plan to try alligator again.

The local Indians came and did ceremonial dancing in beautiful outfits in every color under the sun. They invited John and me to dance with them. The dancing, tribal music, hypnotic beating of the drums, and singing of Indian songs was a little too much for us. We liked to watch, but we didn't join in.

I wish I had a chance to taste the Native American food. When I smelled the delicious smell of Indian cornbread, I figured it might take the nasty taste of alligator out of my mouth.

Cypress Gardens

Another interesting place John and I visited in Florida was Cypress Gardens. We went on a boat ride down a river. Flowers bloomed everywhere and were so brilliant with many colors. The parrots and other birds sang happy songs to us. How amazing the way God had blended in the colors that complemented each other. There were many different kinds of beautiful trees swaying in the breeze, offering their shade. They made me think of how we will eat of the Tree of Life in heaven some day. What a wonderful world God has created, and now John and I were enjoying it. We don't want to miss heaven because we've missed it all if we do.

Ponce Inlet Lighthouse

Another one of my favorite places in Florida was Ponce Inlet Lighthouse. I was shocked the first time we went there. Something near the lighthouse caught my attention. It was a very crude small homemade boat. We were told about Cuban refugees the authorities had recently taken off this small boat. Sometimes when the refugees reached land they would drop down and kiss the ground. Many times these small crudely made boats wrecked and never reached land.

How proud I am to be an American. Land of the free. God bless America. Ponce Inlet Lighthouse has been there many years with its light shining and guiding ships around the treacherous rocks to safety.

I'll never forget going to the top of a lighthouse. The wind was blowing hard. John went ahead of me and was looking out over the ocean. I put my brakes on quickly. I just couldn't make my feet take another step up the winding staircase. John stopped climbing when he realized I wasn't behind him. He looked back at me and started laughing. He knew I couldn't go any farther. He told me to be careful. I started making my way back down those narrow winding steps to solid ground. The breathtaking view of the ocean and sky had been definitely worth the climb. Too bad I hadn't made it the whole way.

We saw a huge anchor there. Every time I looked at it I thought of one of our favorite songs, *The Anchor Holds*. The lighthouse keeper's house was on the grounds near the lighthouse. It has been converted into a gift shop. I found many lighthouse treasures there. The gift shop was always changing the stock, and I was delighted to add to my collection every time we visited. We visited every chance we got since it was my favorite place.

At our house in Ohio, I have a special bedroom I call my Lighthouse Room. I was looking forward to getting wallpaper for that room. God supplied it in the most unexpected way. Not long after our trip to the lighthouse, John and I went to a yard sale. I spied rolls of red wallpaper on a table. I picked up a roll of the paper and felt it was the perfect wallpaper for my lighthouse room. John thought there was enough paper to do my room so we bought every roll on the table.

One day when we got back to Ohio we decided to paper my room. How joyful we were to have a new white ceiling. I painted the woodwork white and the furniture white. Then the Lord blessed us to find a light gray carpet. Later a dear friend of ours, Evelyn Zornes, took me to visit our artist friend who lived near Hillsboro. Truby Abbott was the artist who painted the mural at our church and the picture on the front window. Many of his paintings hung on display at his home. Evelyn told me I could choose any painting I wanted for my birthday gift that year.

I was so excited and in art heaven. It took quite a while to see each painting Mr. Abbott had for sale. My eyes finally landed on a very unusual lighthouse painting. The painting was of a lighthouse on a shore with its light shining out to a ship battling a storm. It even had a white frame that matched my room.

Evelyn asked, "Are you sure that's the one you want?"

"Yes, I am," I told her. It was one of the best birthday gifts I ever received, and I treasure it to this day.

That winter while still in Florida, I wanted to find a bedspread for my lighthouse room back in Ohio. I had started quilting the first winter we went to Florida. My sister-in-law Ruth Powell was the one who stirred my interest in quilting, and I loved it.

While John and I were shopping in Summerfield, Florida I saw some material with lighthouses on it. Hurriedly I purchased the material. My hands stayed busy that winter putting the quilt together and adding a red border. It is still on the bed in my lighthouse room.

Lighthouse paintings by Marjorie Reed

***

The squirrels in Florida were so tame, John would feed them peanuts out of his hand. Every time he went outside the squirrels came running. They always kept an eye out for him.

One of our favorite activities in Florida was going to flea markets. There were so many! John and I always had a good time visiting them. Our last trip to a flea market in Florida, though, was not a good experience.

John had been quiet all morning. Finally he admitted he wasn't feeling well. Not long after that, he vomited into a trashcan. He sat on a bench and leaned against me. Someone near us called 9-1-1. We heard them announce over the P.A. system that someone was sick in our aisle. My cousin Olive, her son Michael, and her husband Paul were also at the flea market that day. They couldn't believe their eyes when they saw it was John who was sick. When the ambulance arrived and checked John out, they decided to take him to the hospital. I rode with him in the life squad to Ocala Hospital. Paul drove our car back to the house.

The doctors at the hospital believed John had a stroke. People looked upside down to him, as if they were walking on the ceiling. I called my brother, George, to tell him what had happened. He offered to bring Mary down to help us. After the doctors completed more tests on John, they didn't want him to leave the hospital. But I insisted we take him home to Hillsboro to see his doctor there.

Ethel May and her husband were looking to buy a house in Florida at this time. Again God's timing was perfect. We sold them our Florida home. Some of our neighbors in Florida, Vern Winkle and his wife Karen, helped us make flight arrangements and prepare to come back to Ohio.

Once we got back to Ohio, John's heart specialist said John needed another heart surgery. John thought and prayed about it. Finally he said he hated to have another surgery, but he would if it was for the best. God was faithful and never left our sides through this very difficult time.

***

Crafts

Our lives settled down after we sold our house in Florida and came back to Ohio. I guess it was good since John and I were ready to relax and enjoy our time together anyway. I had always loved working on crafts, and it was so nice to have time to spend on my crafting hobbies.

I believe my love for doing crafts came from my mother and grandmother. John gave me some saw blades he had cleaned and sanded. This opened a door for me to try another creative outlet. I would go into my own little world as I painted scenes on the saw blades.

Eventually I started making clocks out of circular blades. After I finished the painting, John would put the numbers and clockworks on for me. Lucky for me to have married a carpenter. Jesus knew what it was to be a carpenter, and I married one. John sure was always a blessing to me. Of course I had to paint some lighthouses to add to my collection. Our daughter, Mary, also loves to paint, and she is very talented.

I used to get together with some friends of mine, Lela and Mary Cooper, to make dolls from men's white socks. After we finished, we would display them together. No two were ever exactly the same. Some ended up with big heads and some with little heads. We would laugh so hard at the sight of them until we almost cried. Most of all, we enjoyed each other's company.

I have always loved to quilt. I quilted through the years and only stopped when my eyes would no longer cooperate. I got more adventurous as my skills improved. I wanted to try my hand at a necktie quilt. So the call and search went out for neckties. I was able to get some from each side of the family, which was very special to me, and interesting too. Each necktie was different in color and pattern. It took quite a while to finish one of these special quilts for each of my grandsons.

***

The honeymoon continues

Our daughter Lois and her husband James, who was also my brother, moved to California. She wanted us to be able to say we'd been to California. They sent us plane tickets so we could visit them. It was such an exciting adventure. I had never been on a plane and had never been as far as California.

When we boarded the plane, I took the window seat. John didn't want to sit by the window, but I wanted to see everything I could. I didn't want to miss a thing. When we reached San Diego, I was amazed the buildings were so tall. The plane flew between them, and it looked like we would hit them. It made me very nervous. I couldn't help myself, I held my feet up. John thought it was so funny.

There was a little girl who sat in the same row with us. I talked to her about Jesus and other things. As she got up when it was time to disembark, she said to her mother, "I finally know who Jesus is."

It's a privilege to have an impact on children's lives. It's part of their training, but so many people have forgotten it. I'll never forget that little girl or what she said.

At the San Diego Zoo we saw a huge white python. I was shocked by the length and size of it. All I wanted to do was get out of there. That night I had a nightmare about that snake getting in bed with me. The next morning I was still shook up about it. It was horrible.

John wanted to ride a camel while we were at the zoo. We thought he was kidding so we didn't take the time to do it. After we got back to the house, he said he was really serious about it. I felt bad that he didn't get to ride the camel.

James asked John if he had ever seen a banana split too big to eat. John laughed and said, "No, I've never seen a banana split I couldn't eat."

James took us to an ice cream parlor that served banana splits that weighed five pounds. John managed to eat his, but I couldn't. That banana split was nearly as big as I was.

Lois and James also lived in Arizona for a while, and we went to visit them there. While we were there, we visited the Grand Canyon. Lois would run to the edge of the cliff, but I was too afraid. I never liked heights. When I was growing up in Oregonia, my brothers would climb onto a high bridge and jump off into the Little Miami River. I made sure they never figured out I was afraid, but I stuck to the middle of the bridge so they wouldn't know. Needless to say, the Grand Canyon was more than I could take. I couldn't believe it. It was too much for me. It was beautiful in a way, but in another way, it was scary.

My favorite parts of the Grand Canyon were the historical aspects, the Indian dwellings, and rock outcroppings with the goats. Those goats were braver than me, jumping from rock to rock without a care in the world. While we were there, we found a chapel in the side of a cliff. John and I went to the altar to pray. When we came out it was so beautiful, it reminded me of standing on holy ground.

John's declining health made it difficult for him to move around the way he used to. James and Lois made sure we were able to take our time and enjoy ourselves without feeling rushed or as though we were inconveniencing our hosts.

A Favorite Place

As life here was changing, John and I only drove to places close to home. He teased me and said he was driving Mrs. Daisy. A favorite place of ours to eat was Ponderosa. You know what they say about preachers and their chicken.

Ponderosa was a close drive for us, and the food was delicious. We enjoyed going there as often as we could. We would say our prayers, and generally shortly after that, we'd see Andrea, the owner, coming to our table with a big smile of welcome on her face. We would talk with her a while and always went home happy and blessed. She is one of a kind.

Eventually the time came when John didn't feel comfortable driving at all. Mary usually drove us wherever we needed to go, but I decided to help out as best I could. One day we went shopping. I was behind the wheel, and it was time to go home. As I backed the car out of the parking space, *Wham!* Oh, no! I hit another car.

I was reminded of a song we used to sing: *It's me again, Lord. I got a prayer that needs an answer.*

I sure was praying then. The man whose car I hit sure was a hothead. He said I knocked his car a foot. I was really sorry this happened. His bumper wasn't hurt as far as I could see, but our car had a dent. Fortunately, our grandson, Justin, knew just what to do. He popped out the dent as easy as you please. That was one of my Life Lessons.

CHAPTER TWENTY

A sample of writings I've done through the years

He that dwelleth in the secret place of the Most High shall abide under the shadow of the Almighty. ~Psalms 91:1

The Secret Place

Written September 19, 2001

As a child I had a secret place to read my Bible and pray.
It was under a grove of paw paw trees. I would spread a blanket on the ground and lay.

As I opened my Bible, I would ask God to guide my life that day.
Sometimes the Lord would feel so close.

When I was troubled or maybe felt guilty for something, the Lord seemed so far away.

I'd pray and ask forgiveness as the tears rolled down my face,
Until a peace would cover me as I sought God in my secret place.

The years have come and gone so fast. Wherever I am,

I want to love the Lord and serve him with all my heart.

Yet I knew that God expected me to do my part.

Hold On and Trust

Lord, I need something from you today. Things here have happened that I never thought would come my way.

The battles seem to get longer; my flesh feels so weary I can hardly take one step more. It's then I cry out to you, Lord, for I've never been this way before.

I look for your footprints. They are almost covered over with dust. Then like a cool breeze I hear you whisper my name and say, "Hold on, my child, and trust."

I thought about your disciples in that terrible storm on the Sea of Galilee. Their ship was tossed and the waves loomed high. I think they felt like me.

Just when things looked their worst, and their lives would be lost,
Like us, many times they didn't recognize Jesus.

> *And we know that all things work together for good to them that love God to them who are called according to his purpose.* -Romans 8:28

They Call Me Mom

What a privilege and honor God gave to me, to be the mother of four lovely daughters and one son Tommy.

My life was different from many a mother. But I would not change my life for any other.

My Encounters with Angels

The day I married my John Tom, I became an instant Mom.

Lois was only three. She told everyone I was her new mommy.

We loved each other from the start. She always played the big-sister part.

Leona was eighteen-months-old and just learning to walk. She jabbered more than talk.

She picked the bottom roses off our wedding cake. Got as many as her little fat hands could take.

I prayed earnestly before taking the role of mother and wife. Help me, Oh, God! Guide me in molding each life.

Over two years later God gave us another little girl. With pretty blue eyes and hair that was determined to curl.

Mary Owenna, named after both her grandmothers. She had some of both their ways, some days one and some days the other.

1952 on a beautiful Easter morn, in the hills of Blue Creek. A little son Thomas Clark was born, so precious and sweet.

God loaned him to us for only nine months to stay. He brightened our lives with his sweet dimpled smiles. It was so hard to give him up that cold January day.

Heaven became more real, and I felt its strong pull. Thank you, Heavenly Father, for giving us this little one whose life was so short yet so full.

The Lord knew how empty our arm's felt. Many times we felt our hearts would melt.

Then God in His own special time way, blessed our home with little Rebecca Rose on that snowy 24th of November day. Never was a baby more welcomed by three older sisters cuddling and watching her coo and play.

With four little girls my days were quite full. I'll never forget when she let Daddy her first tooth pull.

She wasn't sure what that string in her daddy's hand would do. He assured her it would all be over before she could say Boo. But who was fooling who?

There were many times of laughter and times of tears. Yet it was worth it all as I look back over the years.

I washed a lot of dirty little faces, and kissed a lot of hurt places.

I've watched each of our girls grow up and bloom. Like a beautiful bouquet, seems it all happened so soon.

One by one they left our little home, to start families of their own.

Blessing our lives again with grandchildren all so sweet. All nine are so special, the finest bunch you could ever meet.

Now we are the proudest grandparents this world can know. Proudly we watch the children's lives flourish and grow.

But none of this could have happened you see, if God had not given my girls to me.

I'm so proud when I hear them call me Mom even today. Each one has a special part in my heart forever to stay.

My Encounters with Angels

My Mother's Hands

Written in honor of my mother on January 10, 1979 at my winter home in Summerfield, Florida.

While doing dishes this morning, I thought of those dear hands of yours. Always so beautiful to me. I thought of the many tears they brushed away. They weren't always tears from your family or friends, which were many, but so often they were your own. You complained so little and smiled through those tears many times. I felt no one was braver than the mother God gave me!

I can almost taste those good biscuits you'd make. I can see you in my mind with your bib apron on, bending over your biscuit board, kneading with those precious hands of yours. You seemed to know just how many handfuls of flour and other ingredients it would take. Oh, Mom, no one could make biscuits as good as yours! Your yeast rolls, loaves of bread, lemon cake, cream and pumpkin pies too! I wish I could have been more like you.

Your hands washed a lot of little dirty faces every day and scrubbed our clothes on a washboard with lye soap your hands had made. In the winter months, you would hang those heavy overalls on the clothesline. They would freeze until they were stiff as a board. Your hands looked so red and cold when you brought them inside.

But finally, the day came that your older brother, Charles Steffy, helped you get an old wooden washer. Now we felt so proud of it and enjoyed helping you wash by pulling that wooden handle back and forth. I think I was about ten-years-old. In the summer you would set it out under our big Catalpa trees. Herbert and George helped too. But even the old sturdy wooden washers could only take so much!

I remember how hard you worked in the fields with Dad to help feed your growing family. It seemed your hands were never idle. Dad rested until you got dinner ready. You worked from daylight until dark. I took care of the little ones. It seemed like there was always a little one to cuddle on your lap. But err the sun began to sink low, you would gather us all in and reach for your Bible, opening its pages ever so tenderly. We would all get quiet as you read God's dear words to us. Then it was time to pray. We knelt on our knees and prayed, thanking God for another day.

Every night you would take down your long dark hair and braid it into one long beautiful braid. You looked so pretty to me. No 'queen' on earth was more beautiful than my mom who God gave to me. You had such a true inward beauty that just seemed to glow on your face at times.

Many people turned to you for help. The kind of help that only God could give them. You would travail in prayer for each one until God sent the answer their way. Just his loving touch of your hand always seemed to mean so much. Your smile went along with each handshake to others. And for you to put your hand in mine or on my shoulder, it just seemed to make everything right again.

Let me mention how God blessed and anointed you to preach his gospel. You may not have been schooled as a great orator, but the great love of God flowed from you as you, in your own simple way, expounded God's word. He gave you such insight on prophecy. He dealt with you in dreams about it as a child even before you learned to read. When you got older and were able to read, you recognized while reading the Bible the same things that had been in your dreams. Through this, God opened your understanding of prophecy to enable you to teach others.

I'd feel the power of God each time you raised your hands, and your face glowed as you magnified God. You always got your sermons while you were on your knees. Only God knows how many souls you won for the Lord. Lives were turned around and they found this wonderful way to start anew.

I can almost see you sitting down at the piano at the little Meadow Run church near Waverly, Ohio. Your hands could only play chords, but everyone would join in singing these old time hymns, clapping their hands and praising God! God's power came down and oh, how we praised the Lord!

I remember you and me singing, *Let me walk with you, Jesus*, before I was married while you would chord on the piano. Yes, these are all precious memories indeed.

My younger brothers never experienced those hands of corrections like we older ones did. Arthritis began to take its toll on those hands. Yes, you guided our lives according to God's Word. Training us up in the way we should go.

Mom, if you could only see us all now. We've all made mistakes, but the same God you taught us to love and serve, has helped us to our feet many times by reaching down his big hand to us. Some of my brothers have gone so deep into sin. I pray for each of them daily. I know they cannot help but miss you at times and remember the way you taught us. I remind God many times in my prayers how he gave you the assurance on the last day of your life when you held my hand inside that oxygen tent in Columbus that he would bring them in. Your face shone with a heavenly glow that day.

You knew you were so near home! Heaven seemed to shine through you. Your joy and happiness was so apparent, I couldn't be sad either. I remember how you said the Lord had called your name that morning, and that you knew he was going to take you home. You sang songs of praise. I can't find words to express how the Glory of God filled that hospital room that day.

You wanted me to put my hand through the oxygen tent so you could hold my hand. I felt your love flow through me as you squeezed my hand. May 30, 1962 was the last day I would ever feel your hand holding mine. It's a day I will always treasure! You left me so much that the world can never give. I still miss you. Like today, I have to take these old hands of mine and brush the tears away from my eyes.

I know you want me to keep my small hands in those big loving hands of Jesus that bore the nail prints for all of us. He is guiding and leading us toward the heavenly home you used to tell us about. I can hardly wait sometimes!

Christmas Eve on Muntz Street

Yes, it's Christmas Eve at our house. The snow is softly falling outside as I look out the window. The birds seem to be having a good time at the bird feeders. The squirrels are eating cracked corn under the walnut tree. Molly, my cat is in the chair beside me washing herself nice and clean.

Princess, our little dog is in her bed snoring away. Our Mary just took a cake out of the oven. Yum. Does it ever smell good. John decided to exercise on his bike. After he turned on the lights in our wreath in the window he set our old nativity scene on the stereo.

Instant Mom

March 11, 1989

Always learning

As a mother I have tried to teach our children right and be the example of a Godly mother. I pray I succeeded in molding their lives by pointing them in the right direction to face life with all the problems, pleasures, etc. Little did they realize they were teaching me many lessons too. Experience is such a good teacher. As a mother, you experience a lot while raising the little ones God entrusted in your care.

The day John and I married I became an instant mom. Lois was three and Leona was only eighteen months, and had just started to talk. I prayed earnestly for God to help me be a good mother. I know I made many mistakes, but I kept trying and praying for wisdom. One day I had a problem I didn't know how to deal with. I sought God's face and he spoke to me. "They are thine and mine," he said. "Guard them diligently."

I'll never forget this. I felt a special bond that he would be my helper and we would share the responsibility of raising them together. Oh, how I loved my girls and I always will. Then God added to our family. Mary Owenna, Thomas Clark, and Rebecca Rose. Our lives have been so full and very rewarding.

Train up a child in the way he should go and when he is old, he will not depart from it.

A Veteran's Prayer—dated July 17, 1999

I wrote this prayer at the request of Vernon Winkle who was doing a presentation for veterans in Hillsboro. I would like to dedicate it to my brothers; George, James, Johnny, and Tim, and to all those who served with honor and valor for our country.

Let us bow our heads and hearts, oh, God.
As we give you thanks for allowing us to gather together again this day.
Let us not forget those who made the ultimate sacrifice.
How you kept your mighty hand over each of us as we fought for our country and the freedom we all enjoy now, making this day possible.
Let us rejoice and be glad in it.
You hold our future in your hands; Help us to use each day wisely.

Guide us, heavenly Father, as we fight the battle of life that lies ahead.

Then when we have fought our last battle here and we stand before you, let it be our greatest homecoming day.

We ask this all in your name, Amen

The following poem was written by Margaret Wilkinson. She was a cousin of mine through marriage. During the summer, we both spent a lot of time on our Aunt Marie's farm. It was generally during canning season when Aunt Marie had plenty of chores to keep kids busy. At Aunt Marie's house, everyone had to work. Margaret was older than me and tried to be a big sister. Sometimes she got a little bossy, but I loved her anyway. Our paths continued to cross as we grew older. While John and I lived in Florida, Margaret and her husband Jim would come down for the winter. Margaret and I often took walks together and got to know each other again. During one of these walks, Margaret presented me with the following poem. At the insistence of my writing partners, Mary Owenna Reed and Teresa Slack, I would like to share it here.

Reflections of Marjorie

She walks in quiet grace with a gentle air,
She greets you with a tender touch and softly whispered prayer.

Like a brightly glowing ember, the Love of God burns bright,
Within the frail human covering, a receptacle of his light.

God gave her John T. as a helpmeet, to share her troubles and strife,
For times of pain and of pleaure, all within the pathways of life.

My life has touched hers often over the passing of the years,
Sometimes we meet in laughter and sometimes we meet in tears.

But the bonds of love and friendship deepen as time goes by,
Tempered with love and prayers we never question why.

My Encounters with Angels

So walk on in faith, dear Marjorie, you do not walk alone,
God's Glory shines around you like light rays from the sun.

Allow not your feet to stumble or question yet the way,
We have his eternal promise, we'll share with him--one day!
God Bless!!!

Margaret Wilkinson
March, 1988

CHAPTER TWENTY-ONE

My beautiful bouquet--our girls

Whenever we would have a family dinner or gathering and I would see our four girls sitting together, I would imagine them as a beautiful bouquet God had given to me. Each girl was lovely and different. I was so blessed to watch them blossom into fine women, and so proud to be their mother. I want to use the next few pages to write a little about each one and the wonderful extended family God gave me.

John and Marjorie's daughters. From left, Mary Reed, Lois Powell, Leona Huddleston, Rebecca Larsen

Lois Marilyn—born September 28, 1944

Our daughter Lois married her sweetheart who was also my brother, James Arnold Powell, at the Carmel Church of God on

My Encounters with Angels

February 28, 1965. It was a beautiful sunny day for a winter wedding. The cake was decorated in pink and white, the bride's favorite colors. Lois's bridesmaids were her best friend Olive Powell and her sister Leona. Jerry Crosswell was James's best man, after whom they named their youngest son Jerry.

Everything about the ceremony was beautiful and memorable. Marlon and Ruth Steffy did the music and songs, which filled the sanctuary with a beautiful melody. The wedding gown had been ordered from Montgomery Ward. Everyone agreed Lois was more beautiful than any model in the catalog. James never looked happier. He got the girl of his dreams.

Behind the scenes, things didn't go so smoothly. Aunt Marie wanted to make sure the wedding night was memorable. Or maybe *she* wanted to be the one nobody forgot. Lois had bought a blue chiffon nightgown and robe set for her wedding night. Aunt Marie sneaked into Lois's bedroom and tied the chiffon gown and robe into knot after knot after knot. She tied those knots as tight as her fingers could manage. That night when Lois went into the bathroom to dress for bed, she was horrified. It seemed to her like hours before she could undo those seemingly endless knots.

Her fingers shook with nervousness and anxiety as she thought of James waiting for her in the next room while she fought those knots. When she finally got the knots out, she saw her lovely chiffon night set was wrinkled beyond repair. She tried everything she could think of to repair the damage, but she couldn't get the wrinkles out. It was a long time before she got up the nerve to come out of the bathroom. James had begun to think she'd jumped out the window.

They got a big laugh out of Aunt Marie's prank later. However, that night Lois did not think it was funny.

James served his country as an M.P. in the Army. James and Lois worked for GM and retired from there. James was an avid golfer. There is a golf tournament in Arizona named after him, which is still played every year.

James and Lois had two sons. Their oldest, James Gregory Powell, was named after his father. Everyone calls him Greg. Once when Greg was small, Lois dropped him off at our house on Muntz Street while she went to work. Our neighbors at the time were the Naylors who had twin girls. Greg was determined to impress those girls.

When Lois came in from work that day, she came inside to talk with me. Little did we know what Greg was about to do. We thought the kids were outside playing with their toys so we planned to enjoy our visit. As soon as Lois went inside and could no longer see them, Greg and the girls climbed into Lois's car. Greg climbed behind the wheel and began going through the motions he had seen his parents do. He shifted gears and began to drive. Our house is on an incline so the car started rolling down the hill. Greg turned the wheel sharply and went right into the Naylors' yard. He wiped out the girls' swing set and some of their toys before the car came to a stop.

The girls screamed as loud as they could. Lois and I heard them from inside the house. We ran outside to see what was going on. The sight of Lois's car in the Naylors' yard with three little kids inside sure scared us too. I guess that was the wildest ride any of them ever had.

Greg retired from the Army. While on active duty, he served in Germany, Korea, Bosnia and two tours in Iraq.

One time Greg and his wife Annette brought their dog Max with them for a visit to our home. Greg had trained Max very well. That morning Greg gave Max the command to go out to get our morning paper. Max completed the order with pride. Watching him in action was something to see.

Greg's wife Annette is so sweet and fits right into our family. The two of them live in Pueblo, Colorado.

Greg has a daughter, Marilyn Kay Powell. Marilyn was named after her grandmother. She has a son Trinidad James Cruz whom she showers with love. She gave us a beautiful, great-great granddaughter this year, named Abigail Renee Cruz. Marilyn wants her children to know our side of the family, and we are all for that.

Greg also has a stepdaughter, Tiffany Marie Trujillo. The first thing I noticed about Tiffany was her eyes. They were the most beautiful brown eyes I'd ever seen. What a brown-eyed beauty she is. We love her so much.

Lois's younger son, Jerry Keith Powell, was a very adventurous little boy. When he was small, I babysat for him sometimes while his parents worked. I kept a special box of toys at my house for the grandkids to play with whenever they came to visit. Jerry was always finding something to play or mischief to get into. When he thought I wasn't looking he would put his bike onto the couch and climb up on it. I thank the Lord he never fell off. Jerry had a poodle named Blackie. Jerry liked to tease Blackie. Blackie liked to play with Jerry and bark at him. Jerry had blond hair and blue eyes. He was all boy and always kept me on my toes. He is now a veterinarian's assistant.

***

Leona Grace Irene—born December 12, 1946

On December 17, 1964, just five days after her eighteenth birthday, Leona followed her heart and eloped to Kentucky with her fiancé Jim Smith. I cried that whole day. But we soon realized Leona and Jim were happy together, and we became happy for them. Leona gave us our first grandchild, a beautiful little girl they named Jonda Jean after John and me.

Jonda was such a delight from the very beginning. With every little whimper or cry out of her mouth, all of us would hurry to see who could get to her first. John always said, "Those girls don't let the baby rest."

Leona also had a stepdaughter named Rita Smith. She was a loving and kind child. Absolutely beautiful, inside and out. Her dark hair and eyes captivated everyone with love the moment they saw her. The last time I saw Rita at church she looked like an angel. I remember watching her pray, and her tears looked like diamonds on her cheeks. When Rita was only nine-years-old, she became very sick. Around three or four o'clock one morning, she called for Leona and told her she was sick. Leona helped Rita to the bathroom. When she led Rita back to bed, the little girl lost consciousness. Leona woke Jim up. He immediately went for his mother. The three adults loaded Rita into the car to take her to the hospital. Jim's mother held Rita as they rushed to the hospital. Tragically, she died before they arrived. Doctors ruled her death from kidney failure.

Leona is an all-around multi-talented person. From the beginning of her marriage to Jim, she worked on the farm with him and helped him in every way. One day while they were working in timber, Jim was wrenching a big log up a hill. The cable hooked to the log broke and whipped backward. It struck Jim in the back. The force of the impact from the cable was so strong, it burst the main artery to Jim's heart. He turned his head toward Leona, but she couldn't do anything. Jim immediately died. It was a very hard time for the family.

Two years after Jim's death, Leona met and married Mark Huddleston.

Diary entry June 24, 1990

John and I are on the road to Kentucky for Leona and Mark's wedding. The sun is shining. What a nice day. It is also John's birthday. I know he enjoyed the wedding cake even though it had no birthday candles. Mary and her family are coming too. The church was decorated very pretty. Leona wore a pink dress and frilly pink hat. She was a beautiful southern belle bride. Mark will make a loving husband. He works hard at BR Retreading, and is a hardworking husband. His hobby is training horses and mules. He has shown them in parades and won a lot of trophies with them.

Leona's daughter, Valynn Lee, served in the Navy. Like many others in the family, she is an accomplished artist. She has painted murals and much more. She is an art teacher in Scottsville, Kentucky. Her classroom is the most colorful room in the building. Valynn married Dale Spearman, and they have two beautiful and talented daughters, Tomorra and Valynncia, who are very supportive of each other.

Leona's youngest daughter, Valerie Irene, always loved animals. When she was very little, John and I took Leona and the girls to the zoo. Valerie reached out to pet a llama and said,

"Don't bite me, doggie."

She always said she wanted to be a veterinarian when she grew up. She worked very hard while in college, and her hopes and dreams came true. Valerie is now a veterinarian in Glasgow, Kentucky. The workers at the clinic recognize she has a special gift with animals, especially horses. They call her the 'Horse Whisperer'. Once I asked her what was the most unusual animal she had treated. I was shocked when she said a giraffe.

Valerie married Ronnie Dale Mosby on a cruise ship. Ronnie was a detective before he retired. Even though Ronnie is retired from his career, he is busy now as a Super Dad to their son Sawyer James. James is a charmer and a delight to all the family.

John and I always looked forward to going to Kentucky to spend time with Leona and her family. One trip, I was especially excited to get there. Valerie had been searching for a dog for us. She found a man who raised Chihuahuas and worked out a deal with him to get me a puppy. When we got there, I couldn't wait to see the puppy. It was a little girl—mostly black with some brown and a little white. John gave Valerie the fifty dollars she had paid. It was a great bargain. I couldn't be happier.

Oh, my, how tiny she was looking up at us, wagging her itty bitty tail. She melted my heart instantly. I was a mother again. I named my new baby Princess. She was so small, John was able to carry her around in his shirt pocket, and I carried her in my apron pocket when I was busy. I didn't think we would, but John and I let her sleep in bed with us that night. It was the first time we ever slept with a dog. But who could ignore those little crying whimpers?

Leona's children are grown now. Her beautiful little girl Jonda Jean married Robert Terry Neal on Valentine's Day, 2000. Jonda is a bright and bubbly person. Everyone loves being around her. She has two step children, Joshua and Nicole. Jonda and Terry live in Texas. Jonda works at Dumas Junior High School. Her heart is working with children.

***

Mary Owenna—born August 2nd, 1950

Mary was a Daddy's girl from the very beginning. She loved to do everything with John. She worked right beside him while building the church. She became a dedicated Sunday School teacher and truly loved the children. She still sings in the choir at the Hillsboro Church of God where John was the pastor.

When she married, she blessed John and me with two grandsons, Justin David and Antiny Owen. Both of them went to college and earned their degrees with high honors.

Mary and Antiny spent a lot of time at our house helping us in many ways. John taught Antiny how to drive while taking him to school. He also taught Antiny to play songs on the mandolin. It was joyful music to my ears. I am so pleased that Antiny chose to follow in his grandpa's footsteps by evangelizing in the ministry. He worked for the court systems and now works for the U.S. Postal Service.

John loved to take the boys fishing when they were young. Justin showed an interest in cars when he was still little. He earned a vocational license in mechanics in high school. He continued his education and earned his degree in diesel mechanics and business at Northwestern in Ohio. He is now a professional at restoring and repairing vehicles. His mom calls him 'Hot Rod'. Justin and his wife Cierra stop in regularly with helpful hearts, doing chores and brightening my day. Both Justin and Cierra work at ABX in Wilmington, Ohio.

Mary has always loved any form of art. She has won many awards, ribbons, and accolades for her paintings and drawings. In one competition, she even won first, second, and third place. I am so proud of her. I like to think she inherited her artistic ability from me, but I know it was the Lord who gave it to her. She has always been such a blessing to John and me by taking care of us and being available any time we need her.

Mary also went to college and earned a degree. When she worked at the Highland District Hospital in Hillsboro, she was able to care for John and me when we were patients there on separate occasions. She also worked with me nearly every day getting this book ready for publication. Anyone who has ever attempted such an undertaking knows all the blood, sweat, and tears that go into it. Every time Teresa and I needed copies or edits or fact checking, Mary was there to help. She brought us lunch for every work session and worked right beside us, making the book the best it could be. The beautiful cover the Lord showed me in my vision was brought to life through Mary and Teresa working together, and not giving up until it was just the way I wanted. I don't believe I could've managed this daunting project without Mary's support and hard work.

Our Father Who Art in Heaven.
Drawn by Mary O. Reed.

Marjorie J. Reed

***

Rebecca Rose

Time went by and our nest kept getting emptier. When Rebecca graduated from high school, the Lord let us know she should further her education. We were able to send her to Lee College in Cleveland, Tennessee for two years. There she met her future husband, John Michael Larsen. He was a ministerial student from Oregon.

I decided to make my dress for their wedding. Her colors were red and white. I ordered red and white material and bought a pattern to make a floor length dress with long sleeves. This brought back memories of my Grandma Steffy making Mom's wedding dress years ago. So many things were happening, and with all the excitement over the wedding plans, I broke out all over with hives and had to make a trip to the doctor.

Mike's parents and his sister, who live in Oregon, were coming in for the wedding, along with a brother from Canada and another from Emory University in Georgia. We had not met any of them yet. Maybe that's why I was so nervous.

Mary offered her wedding dress to her little sister to wear. Our friend Aurela was a good seamstress and she began making alterations right away on the dress. John and I bought Rebecca a new long flowing veil to wear because Mary's veil had touched a candle during her wedding ceremony and had a scorched place on it.

The alterations were finally finished. Rebecca anxiously tried on her dress. How beautifully picture perfect she was. She looked so lovely. My eyes got a little teary at the sight of her. My baby was now a lady.

The Hillsboro Church of God had just laid down new red carpet that morning. It was a perfect match for Rebecca's wedding colors. How beautiful the sanctuary looked for her wedding. John and I were happy and proud of the church and our church family.

A dear friend of ours, Brother Orville Morgan, who was also a pastor, had teased Rebecca many years earlier about performing her wedding ceremony. Wouldn't you know it, he was still able to officiate at the ceremony.

Everything about the church was beautiful for their wedding. Michael and Rebecca's faces were aglow with the light from the candles around them. As I looked on from my spot beside John, I couldn't help wondering where the years had gone. Even Brother Morgan had a special smile on his face.

I must tell you about Rebecca's special wedding cake. Remember her name…Rebecca Rose. Well, we ordered a cake with white icing, decorated with red roses. This was so appropriate, and it tasted so good.

At the end of the reception when it came time for the traditional tossing of the garter and bouquet, Rebecca and Mike experienced a communication failure. Rebecca leaned over to him and asked if he was ready to toss the garter. Mike looked at her with a look of total shock on his face.

"Here?" he said loud enough for everyone around them to hear.

In turn, Rebecca was very embarrassed by his reaction. She said, "Well, where do you think I've got it?" By then both of them were so embarrassed and red-faced, they decided to skip that part of the ceremony.

After the reception, we came back to our house. My dad asked Rebecca to play a song on the piano and sing for him before she and Michael left for their honeymoon. After everyone had left the house, it was very quiet. John put his arms around me. It's a day I will never forget. Now I knew what it was to say all my children were gone.

Marjorie at Rebecca's wedding, wearing the red dress she made for the occasion. Pictured from left; Rebecca, Mary, Leona, Lois, Marjorie and John.

Before I go on in the story I'd like to give God praise and glory. I must tell a quick story about Brother Morgan. When I was only eight-years-old, I felt led of the Lord for Brother Morgan to baptize me. I wanted to be and do whatever God wanted of me so I could go to heaven. The water in the Little

Miami River was muddy so you couldn't see through it. On the day of my baptism, the current was pretty strong.

While Brother Morgan was immersing another person into the water for baptism, his glasses got knocked off. Brother Morgan asked the Lord to help him find his glasses. We kids and the adults standing by were all eyes to see what would happen. We watched Brother Morgan and prayed with him that the Lord would help him retrieve his glasses from the muddy water.

God did. Brother Morgan reached right into that muddy water and scooped up his glasses like they were just waiting for him to get them. We all started shouting and rejoicing with him for finding his glasses.

What an awesome God we serve. Brother and Sister Morgan served as pastor for the Church of God. They served the Lord wholeheartedly and brought many to know the Lord. Everyone loved them.

***

Years after Michael and Rebecca married, the Lord called Michael to go to Korea to serve as a missionary. They began to prepare with their girls Charity Faith and Rebecca Hope. At this time the Lord didn't give me any assurance they would come back. I had to trust Him to take care of them no matter what.

I believed Rebecca needed to have her music with her in Korea. John and I decided an accordion would be the best thing. We prayed about it and found an advertisement in the Cincinnati Enquirer. I had some money saved up to buy it. Aunt Marie donated her dime collection to help pay for it, and others also gave us money. When we went to see the accordion, the price was exactly the amount we had to spend. On the way home we sang and praised the Lord for all he had done.

The last time our family got together before Michael and Rebecca left for Korea, we had a special dinner at the Hillsboro Park on Route 50. We presented Rebecca with the beautiful gold and ivory accordion. John played his mandolin, and Rebecca tried out the new accordion. The music blessed all of us and drifted heavenward. I felt as if the angels sang with us.

The day finally came for us to take them to the airport in Chattanooga, Tennessee. Hope clung to my neck. She cried, "I don't want to go. Grandma, let me stay with you."

It was so hard to take her arms away from my neck. Charity had just started kindergarten. Things would really be different for her once she got to Korea. It would be different for us, too, not having them nearby. My heart ached as we said our goodbyes and 'I love you's'. As the plane broke through the clouds, the sun shone on it so vividly. I believe God was trying to encourage us. We wanted his will for all of their lives more than anything else. Michael and Rebecca would be teaching English to Korean military officers and numerous security agents who were bodyguards to the president of Korea. They would also be helping to minister at the Church of God Christian Serviceman's Center near Itaewon Korea, as well as work with Rev. Yeoung Hun Han and the Korean Church of God.

Upon arrival in Korea their suitcases were inspected. It turned out the accordion had a special mission too. At the airport the inspector wanted to know what it was. He had never seen an accordion. He was finally convinced it was okay to let them keep it.

Each month the Korean Army Language Training Center where Mike and Rebecca taught English had a special introduction party for new classes and another for graduating classes. Rebecca was asked to sing so she took her accordion with her to perform for them. Everyone who heard it loved the music.

She felt she should sing: *He's still working on me.* From then on she brought her accordion every month and sang Christian songs while praying the Holy Spirit would touch the hearts of those who heard her. The accordion performed its mission as long as they were there. We will never know what was accomplished until God rewards them.

My Encounters with Angels

Graduating Class #20 of the Republic of Korea Language Training Center. Rebecca is in second row in blue. Mike is next to her in brown suit.

The Korean culture and food were so different from what Rebecca and Mike were used to. On one occasion, Rebecca asked one of the Korean soldiers what kind of soup they were having. It was curdled pork blood! They did not eat that again. On another occasion, a Korean colonel smiled at Rebecca as he dipped his chopsticks into a bowl. He pulled out a sample and held it out to her. "Taste this."

Even though Mike would try anything, Rebecca wasn't so sure. Myung, a Korean-American friend, said, "Eat it, Rebecca. You won't die."

Rebecca didn't want to, but she didn't want to offend her host either. She accepted the bite and quickly swallowed it with a grimace. Only then did they tell her it was sautéed grasshopper.

Larsen family January 1986.

After Rebecca married John Michael, that made three John's in our immediate family...so far! Their daughter, Charity Faith, married another John named John Burke. Their youngest daughter, Rebecca Hope, also married a man whose first name is John. At least his last name is Zavatchen. We only have one of those.

Hope has a stepdaughter Melissa who is married to Brett Bynum. Hope is such a blessing as she sends letters and pictures to us. We check the mailbox often for something from her and all our other wonderful grandchildren and great-grandchildren. It is a delight and helps make the miles between us seem not so far.

I remember when all my grandchildren were born, and Rebecca's girls were no different. As time drew close for her first child to be born, her feet and legs started to swell. John took me to Tennessee to be near her. I wanted to be helpful, so I fixed a meal for the family. I didn't realize Mike had thought ahead and planned each meal. I guess I rearranged that plan.

It was a dark, rainy night when the baby decided it was time to be born, so off to the hospital we went. As morning came, we had a beautiful new granddaughter. I thought she looked like her Grandmother Larsen. Rebecca and Mike named her Charity Faith. Charity calls often. I look forward to hearing from her so much. Each call ends with, "I love you, Grandma."

The day after Valentine's Day many years later, John and I got the call that Charity had given birth to a girl, Audrey Nichole. How happy to have another great-granddaughter. John and I thought of her as our sweet Valentine. We know we have enough love for all our grandchildren and great-grandchildren.

Abigail Reice was Charity's second daughter. She is sweet and petite, just like her Grandma Reed. When her family would come to visit, she would sometimes crawl into my lap and go to sleep.

I remember one day, John and I were sitting in the living room when little Abigail decided to entertain us by reading from a storybook. She really got into telling the story. Her facial expressions and arm and body movements surely had us engrossed in the story. Abigail made the story come to life. I wonder if she will be our next storyteller.

I'll never forget the night Rebecca and Mike's second daughter, Rebecca Hope, was born. It was pouring rain again, just like the night we went to the hospital for Charity. This time, I couldn't find my rain cap. I looked everywhere, but time was getting short, and I really needed it. I found a plastic bag and figured it would work just as well. Over my head it went. Mike gave me a strange look. I could tell he was embarrassed by me using the plastic bag. He picked up his pace so he could walk ahead of me. I guess he didn't want to be seen with a bag lady. I just figured he didn't have as much hair to get wet as I did, and the plastic bag worked just fine.

CHAPTER TWENTY-TWO

When John and I took our marriage vows we said, 'Till death do us part.' John had suffered for a long time. We knew he didn't have much time left. I wanted Hospice to come in so he could be at home when his time came. The last time John left the hospital he told me he felt like it was time to give up and go on to be with the Lord. I couldn't keep the tears back. He didn't want to leave me because he didn't know what would happen to me.

Hospice brought John home where he wanted to be. I was so glad we had come this far in the battle together.

One day while I was holding John's hand and singing to him, he said, "Honey, pray for the Lord to heal me."

I wrapped both my hands around his. "Honey, everything God has asked us to do, we've done it. This time we also have to say, 'Your will be done.' God's will is always best."

Telling John this was the hardest words I ever had to say. I wanted him to be healed more than anything. I wanted him to stay with me for as many years as I had left on this earth. However, I believed what I said. God's will is always best even when it isn't what we want at the time.

I felt such a peace come over me, and I knew it was time. I believe John accepted it too. So many people had been praying for him for eight years. God was hearing and honoring those prayers. John would recover for a time, but then he'd get sick again and have to go through the pain again. It was so hard and stressful for both of us to watch him go back and forth.

Once we were both willing to let God's will be done and for him to finish his work in John's life, the peace came over me. I told John I felt such a peace about this. In the midst of everything, I knew it was time, and John's life was short for this world.

Many times I would just sit in my chair and sing to him. I would tell him over and over, "I love you with my whole heart."

He would say the same words back to me. One beautiful day, Brother King called to ask if he could come over with his guitar and sing while Sister King prepared a meal for us. While I was waiting for the Kings to arrive, I prayed he would sing about heaven to John. I had been singing those songs to encourage John for a long time, but I felt he needed to hear them from someone besides me.

God answered my prayers. When Brother King got to the house, he sang two songs about heaven. It made me feel so good. I believed it wouldn't be long until John would know for himself what Heaven was like.

The Highland District Hospital had home health care workers and Hospice had nurses and aides who came to the house to take care of John. They were very helpful and caring. Cindy was one who brightened our day every time she came. She continues to come even now and there is a special bond of Christian love between us. She washes and fixes my hair for me every Saturday so it will look nice for church on Sunday. Sometimes she and her daughter surprise me with food. Such a blessing they are to our family. John's eyes would brighten every time he saw them come. That meant so much to me.

The doctor and a few of the Hospice nurses told me the sooner I told the girls about John's condition, the better because he wouldn't last much longer. Lois already had a plane ticket to fly in for John's ninetieth birthday, but she was able to make some changes. Thankfully all four of the girls made it to our house in time. John recognized each one of them.

Leona told him, "This is your mean one."

John gave her a smile and said, "No, you are my sweetie pie. I'll always love you."

Mary could hardly say goodbye. She had always been her daddy's girl, and she took his passing so hard. He was holding her hand when he passed away.

I thank God with all my heart that our little family was together for just a few minutes letting him know how much we loved him before he lost consciousness. I will always thank God for this short period we were all together. We knew he was ready when God took him and we're looking forward to that great reunion day. We know he's not suffering anymore and he's with the Lord rejoicing.

Let the words of my mouth and the meditation of my heart be acceptable in your sight, O Lord, my strength and my Redeemer. -Romans 8:28

He went home to be with the Lord on April 7, 2013. His last words to me were, "I love you more than words can say."

Postscript

God has given me such wonderful people, whose support and encouragement have meant so much to me as I worked on this book. I want to mention a few of those encouragers: Evelyn Zornes, Olive Thompson, and Lela Wheeler. I am honored to have such wonderful friends and family. There have been many others that have blessed our lives. God knows each and every one. A special thanks to Mr. and Mrs. Roger Moore for so lovingly making tapes and CD's for us. And I can't forget Community Care Hospice for their kindness and tender loving care to our family during John's passing.

I could not have finished this book without the help of Teresa Slack. I want to thank her for the monumental amount of time and insight she provided throughout the process of making the vision the Lord gave me of this book possible. She has been a beacon of light to me and I highly recommend her books for reading pleasure.

Teresa, you are one of my miracles.

In closing I want to thank each one I've known over the years for their prayers. May God's blessings rest upon each and every person. I pray that in some way this book will be an encouragement to any one who reads it. Just remember, for every valley no matter how deep, there are two mountaintops. I feel this will be my last tribute to my family and friends. I will be looking for you at the Marriage Supper of the Lamb in Heaven.

More than anything I want my last mile to be my best. I know I'm getting close to the end of my life. So many people have told me they believe this book will be special in making my last mile the best I have to offer the Lord. I never would've attempted to write this book for glory for myself. All the glory belongs to my heavenly father.

I don't want to leave anything undone before God takes me home. I want to know I did my best for him. Completing *My Encounters with Angels* is an act of obedience. Doing my best for the Lord has always been the most important thing in my life.

I want to have a clear conscious when I stand before him. I want to have done my all for him. I admonish each of you to leave no job undone. Make sure everything is clear. Walk in obedience all the days of your life. God's ways are always best even when we don't understand them at the time. As long as we trust him in every way, God will be a reflection in your life.

It's worth it.

> *Great is the Lord, and greatly to be praised; and his greatness in unsearchable. One generation shall praise thy works to another, and shall declare thy mighty acts. I will speak of the glorious honor of thy majesty, and of thy wondrous works. And men shall speak of the might of thy terrible acts: and I will declare they greatness.* -Psalm 145: 3-6

Marjorie pictured with Teresa Slack, hard at work on the book.

ABOUT THE AUTHORS

Marjorie J. Reed

Born and raised in southwestern Ohio to loving, godly parents, Marjorie J. Reed is the product of a strong Christian heritage. At a young age, she determined to defy the obstacles in her path and triumph through her tears. Her story is one of strength and the hope she clings to through life's challenges, hardships and tragedies.

Marjorie is the author of hundreds of inspirational poems and devotionals written to encourage and inspire believers and help the lost understand their need for a Savior. Several of her poems and the stories that inspired them are included in her book, *My Encounters with Angels and Other Memoirs*. If God wills, she looks forward to publishing and sharing more of her poems with her readers in the future.

Teresa Slack

Teresa Slack's first novel, *Streams of Mercy*, won the Bay Area Independent Publishers' Association award for Best First Novel. *Evidence of Grace*, the third in her Jenna's Creek Series debuted at #18 nationwide according to Christian Retailing Magazine. Her down-to-earth characters and realistic dialog have endeared her to readers and reviewers alike.

She and her husband Ralph are faithful members of the Hillsboro Church of God where Teresa teaches the preschool Sunday School class and Ralph teaches the adult class. Teresa is crazy busy at work on her next novel, a series of short stories, and her first western.

Learn more about her and her books at her website www.teresaslack.com or on her Facebook author page. Like all writers, she loves hearing from readers. You can contact her at teresa@teresaslack.com Find more of Teresa Slack's books on her Amazon author page: http://www.amazon.com/Teresa-D.-Slack/e/B001JP0MQ2

To order autographed copies of this book, please send payment plus $4.00 shipping and handling to: Mary O. Reed P.O. Box 573, New Vienna, OH 45159. Additional copies can be mailed to the same address with payment, plus an additional $2.00 per copy for shipping.

John and Marjorie on their 64th anniversary, June 4th, 2012

Made in the USA
Charleston, SC
03 July 2016